CONTENTS

40 3/27
CLEARANCE
$ 50

On the Cover (Left to Right):
Rich Buttery Pecan Pie - The Woodstock Inn & Resort; Pecan Molasses Pork Loin with White Cheddar Mashed Potatoes - Olde Mill Inn; Oriental Chicken Quiche - Opryland Hotel; Stuffed Summer Squash - Carter House; Cheddar Cheese Scones - Eagle Ridge Inn & Resort; Rich Blueberry Pancakes - The Inn Above Onion Creek

New England

New England offers a bounty of four seasons of beauty and a rich history that formed the foundation of our country. From its rocky beaches and boat-filled harbors along the coast to majestic mountains surrounded by quaint villages, New England has long been a favorite destination for those seeking to explore our historical roots and sample some of our country's most traditional foods.

The rich culinary history of New England has its origins in both the Native Americans and the earliest European settlers. The Pilgrims landed in Massachusetts in 1620, fleeing from England in search of religious freedom. There, they encountered the Wampanoag natives, who introduced them to corn, squash and beans, and taught them how to hunt, fish and farm. A year after settling in Plymouth, the Pilgrims celebrated their survival with a Thanksgiving feast of venison, wild turkey, oysters, nuts, fruits and vegetables.

A few years later, the first settlers were joined by their fellow Englishmen, the Puritans. Together, they domesticated wild turkey and caught numerous varieties of fish and shellfish. And, in addition to the native crops of corn and beans, they also raised vegetables brought from England such as cabbage, onions and turnips. The Puritans imported dairy and beef cattle from Europe, and also constructed trading ships that made it possible to acquire tea and spices from China; wines, brandy and raisins from the Mediterranean; and molasses from the West Indies.

Eventually, other Europeans made their way to the region, bringing with them their own favorite foods: the Scottish and Welsh brought their recipes for scones and oatmeal breads and introduced leeks to the New England vegetable garden; the Portuguese demonstrated new ways to prepare fish; and the Italians introduced pasta and broccoli. When the French Canadians emigrated to New England, they brought with them recipes for thick, hearty pea soups and pork pies.

But of all its foods, New England is probably best known for its seafood. Due to the harshness and unpredictability of the weather for farming, fish and shellfish made seafood the dominant cuisine of early New England. Hardy fishermen brought loads of fresh seafood to the tables of New Englanders. Fishing became essential to the growing economy and clams, oysters, cod, mackerel and scallops were basic ingredients of many meals.

Today, the evolution of New England cooking has given us the original clam chowder, New England boiled dinner, New England clam bake, the traditional roasted turkey, pumpkin pie and Indian pudding. These early specialties were later joined by such classics as Parker House rolls, Boston cream pie, brownies, fudge, and even the classic chocolate chip cookie!

THE WOODSTOCK INN & RESORT

Woodstock, Vermont

The Woodstock Inn and Resort is located in Woodstock, Vermont, considered by National Geographic magazine to be one of the most beautiful towns in America.

The Woodstock Inn, owned by Mr. and Mrs. Laurance Rockefeller, offers all the charm of the colonial era with all the luxuries and conveniences of today. The 144 rooms and suites, many with fireplaces, are graciously decorated with specially designed furniture and beautiful handmade quilts.

The Inn and Resort offers a range of indoor and outdoor activities. Guests of the Inn have access to a 50-foot pool, 18-hole Robert Trent Jones Sr. Golf Course, bicycle rentals and guided nature walks. The resort offers the guests a range of facilities which include alpine skiing, the Woodstock Ski Touring Center, tennis, health and fitness center, squash, racquetball, paddle tennis and croquet.

The resort offers a variety of restaurants that serve delicious meals throughout the day. The Inn offers unparalleled cuisine and is renowned for its style and service.

The area surrounding Woodstock also offers guests a vast array of interesting places to visit. In the nearby town of Norwich is Vermont's largest science museum with exhibits geared specially to children. The Quechee Gorge, also known as Vermont's "Little Grand Canyon," is located 7 miles east of Woodstock.

A visit to the Woodstock Inn and Resort will insure its guests comfort, a sense of history, and fine cuisine.

NEW ENGLAND CLAM CHOWDER

Yield: 9 (1-cup) servings

- 1 *cup diced onions*
- ¾ *cup sliced celery*
- ⅓ *cup diced salt pork, rind removed, or 3 strips bacon, cut up*
- ¼ *cup (½ stick) butter*
- 1 *tablespoon oil*
- 1 *teaspoon salt*
- ¼ *teaspoon white pepper*
- ¼ *teaspoon dried thyme leaves*
- ¼ *teaspoon paprika*
- 1 *bay leaf*
- ½ *cup all-purpose flour*
- 2 *medium potatoes, peeled, cut into 1-inch pieces*
- 1 *cup water*
- 2 *cups clam juice (8-ounce bottle)*
- 1 *cup shucked clams or 2 (10-ounce) cans clams, drained, reserving liquid*
- ½ *cup cream*

In large skillet over medium heat, cook onions, celery and salt pork in butter and oil. Add salt, pepper, thyme, paprika and bay leaf; cook until vegetables are crisp-tender. Stir in flour until well mixed. Cook about 5 minutes being careful not to burn, stirring constantly.

Meanwhile, in large saucepan, cook potatoes in water, clam juice and reserved clam liquid for about 15 minutes or just until potatoes are tender.

Add clams and onion mixture to potatoes. Cook and stir until mixture is thickened and thoroughly heated. Stir in cream.

Rich Buttery Pecan Pie

RICH BUTTERY PECAN PIE

Yield: 8 servings

- 1 *(10 inch) unbaked pie shell*
- 1½ *cups firmly packed brown sugar*
- ¾ *cup honey*
- ½ *cup (1 stick) butter*
- ¼ *cup heavy cream*
- 4 *cups (1 lb.) pecans*

Heat oven to 350°F. Bake pie shell 10 minutes.

Meanwhile, in medium saucepan, combine brown sugar, honey and butter; mix well. Bring to a boil. Boil 3 minutes, stirring occasionally. Remove from heat; stir in cream and pecans. Pour into partially baked pie shell. Place pie on cookie sheet.

Bake at 350°F for 30 to 35 minutes or until filling is bubbly. Cool completely on wire rack for 1 1/2 to 2 hours before serving.

ACORN SQUASH AND VERMONT APPLE BISQUE

Yield: 8 (1¼-cup) servings

- 2 *pounds acorn squash, peeled, cut into 2-inch pieces*
- 2 *MacIntosh apples, cored, peeled*
- 1 *medium potato, peeled cut into 2-inch pieces*
- 1 *onion, cut into wedges*
- 1 *celery stalk, cut into 1-inch pieces*
- 1 *carrot, cut into 1-inch pieces*
- 1 *garlic clove, finely minced*
- ½ *cup (1 stick) butter*
- 1 *teaspoon chopped walnuts*
- 2 *teaspoons brown sugar*
- 1 *teaspoon maple syrup*
- ⅛ *teaspoon nutmeg*
- ¼ *teaspoon salt*
- ¼ *teaspoon pepper*
- 1 *bay leaf*
- 1 *quart (4 cups) chicken broth*
- 1 *cup apple cider*

In food processor bowl with metal blade, process squash, apples, potato, onion, celery, carrot and garlic until finely minced. Melt butter in Dutch oven. Add vegetable mixture; cook until crisp-tender, stirring frequently.

Meanwhile, in food processor, finely chop walnuts. Add to vegetable mixture; cook about 5 minutes. Add all remaining ingredients. Bring to a boil. Reduce heat; simmer until vegetables are tender. Serve soup topped with whipped cream; sprinkle with cinnamon.

◆ ◆ ◆ ◆ ◆ ◆ ◆ ◆ ◆ ◆

The Key to Great Taste

If you want to get creative in the kitchen, start with butter. No matter what you do, your creations are bound to come out well, because butter makes everything taste better.

◆ ◆ ◆ ◆ ◆ ◆ ◆ ◆ ◆ ◆

DEERFIELD INN

Deerfield, Massachusetts

The Deerfield Inn is located in the heart of the 300 year old village of Old Deerfield, Massachusetts. Old Deerfield is recognized as a National Historic Landmark and known as the "undiscovered" jewel of New England. Settled around 1670, it was once an outpost of Colonial America. Today, Deerfield seems untouched by the progress of history elsewhere in America, and stands as a living example of an Early New England frontier community.

The Inn, built in 1884, is known for its warm, friendly and gracious atmosphere which is enhanced by its collection of lovely period antiques.

The classic New England Inn has 23 rooms each beautifully decorated and named after a person connected with the village's history.

The Deerfield Inn believes that eating well is an important part of enjoying your stay. Its cuisine is continental and its specialty is excellence. Days begin with a hearty country breakfast and end with a candle-lit dinner. Lunch is also served at the Inn and there is an English tea for guests in the afternoon. The kitchen uses the freshest and finest local ingredients, and some of their regional dishes are right out of the old recipe books from the village library. The Inn is renowned for its gracious hospitality and friendly service.

The town of Deerfield offers shopping, antiquing, and 14 museum houses open to the public. The surrounding area also offers such popular tourist destinations as the Bridge of Flowers in Shelburne Falls and The Basketball Hall of Fame in Springfield. Outdoor enthusiasts may enjoy hiking and both cross-country and down-hill skiing.

The Deerfield Inn in the village of Deerfield is a perfect destination for those looking for New England the way they hoped to find it.

MOLASSES COOKIES

Yield: 4-8 dozen cookies

- 2 *cups sugar*
- 1½ *cups (3 sticks) butter*
- ½ *cup molasses*
- 2 *eggs*
- 4 *cups all-purpose flour*
- 1 *teaspoon baking soda*
- ½ to 1 *teaspoon salt*
- 2½ *teaspoons cinnamon*
- 1 *teaspoon ginger*
- 1 *teaspoon cloves*

Heat oven to 350°F. Butter and flour cookie sheets. In large bowl, beat sugar and butter until light and fluffy. Add molasses and eggs; beat well. In medium bowl, combine all remaining ingredients. Add to butter mixture; mix well. For 2-inch cookies, drop dough by rounded teaspoonfuls, or for 4-inch cookies, drop dough by walnut-sized balls onto buttered and floured cookie sheets.

Bake at 350°F for 8 to 10 minutes or until edges just begin to brown. Cool 1 minute; remove from cookie sheets. Cool on wire racks.

Almond Butter Melt-Aways

Almond Butter Melt-Aways

Yield: 12 dozen (1¾-inch) cookies

- 4 *ounces almond paste*
- 3 *cups powdered sugar*
- 4 *eggs*
- 2 *cups (4 sticks) butter*
- 5¾ *cups cake flour*

Heat oven to 375°F. Line cookie sheets with parchment paper. In large bowl, combine almond paste and sugar; beat well.

Add eggs one at a time, beating well after each addition. Add butter; beat until light. Add flour; mix until smooth. With No. 4 star tip, pipe onto paper-lined cookie sheet.

Bake at 375°F for 6 to 8 minutes or until edges are light brown and centers are set. Do not overbake.

Lemon-Orange Pound Cake

Yield: 2 (9-inch) loaf cakes

- 3 *cups sugar*
- 1½ *cups (3 sticks) butter*
- 6 *eggs*
- ¼ *cup heavy cream*
- 4 *tablespoons grated lemon peel*
- 2 *tablespoons grated orange peel*
- 1 *teaspoon salt*
- 3 *cups cake flour*

Heat oven to 350°F. Butter two 9x5-inch loaf pans. In large bowl, combine sugar and butter; beat until well blended. Add eggs, cream, lemon peel, orange peel and salt; mix well. Gently fold flour into butter mixture. Pour half of batter into each buttered pan.

Bake at 350°F for 50 to 60 minutes or until toothpick inserted in center comes out clean. Cool in pan 25 minutes. Loosen edges with metal spatula; remove from pans. Place upright on wire racks; cool completely.

◆ ◆ ◆ ◆ ◆ ◆ ◆ ◆ ◆ ◆ ◆ ◆ ◆

Butter Storage

Store butter refrigerated or frozen, well-wrapped or in a sealed container, and away from vegetables and other highly aromatic foods.

Refrigerated:

- Unopened butter keeps in the refrigerator for several weeks.
- Store opened butter, covered, in the refrigerator butter keeper.

Frozen:

- To freeze butter, seal in a plastic freezer bag or wrap tightly with heavy-duty foil.
- Butter may be frozen up to 9 months.
- For best flavor, store unsalted butter in the freezer until ready to use.

When grating lemon, lime or orange, use only the colored part of the rind. The inner white part is bitter.

◆ ◆ ◆ ◆ ◆ ◆ ◆ ◆ ◆ ◆ ◆ ◆ ◆

Griswold Inn

Essex, Connecticut

The Griswold Inn is located in the charming town of Essex, Connecticut.

The Inn was built in 1776 by Sala Griswold with the promise of providing "first class accommodations" to travelers. Nearly 220 years and six proprietors later, the Inn still lives up to that promise.

Over the years, the Inn has played an important role in local history. During the War of 1812, British mariners destroyed the Essex fleet by fire and proceeded to commandeer the Inn during their Connecticut Valley Campaign. The main building was the first three-story frame structure built in Connecticut. The Tap Room was originally built in 1738 as an Essex schoolhouse which was moved to its present location in 1865 by a team of oxen. "The Covered Bridge Room" was constructed from an abandoned New Hampshire covered bridge moved to Essex in 1946.

The special charm of the "Gris" is enhanced by an extensive collection of steamboat prints and memorabilia as well as an important collection of Courier & Ives and Edicott prints. One of America's largest collections of Antonio Jacobsen marine oils can also be enjoyed at the Inn. The collections have been assembled over nearly two centuries and are considered among the most important American marine collections in private hands today.

The Inn has 7 dining rooms and 27 lovely guest rooms, many with fireplaces.

The Inn is known for its delicious American cuisine using only the freshest ingredients. Many of their specialties include seafood and grilled meats.

Among the many luncheon specials is their famous 1776 sausage made from the Inn's 200 year old recipe.

The charming town of Essex is located on the Connecticut River. Guests can browse through its many shops and visit its Historic Waterfront. The surrounding towns provide attractions such as Mystic Seaport, Olde Mystic Village, Mystic Aquarium, New Haven's Peabody Museum, Hamden's The Goodspeed Opera House as well as the Eugene O'Neil Theater Center in Waterford.

As the Inn changed over the years from a stagecoach - steamboat stop to a Country Inn catering to neighbors, yachtsmen and overland travelers, it has never forgotten its promise of providing first class accommodations and service to its guests.

Oyster Stew with Cream

Yield: 8 (1 ¼-cup) servings

- ¼ *cup oil*
- 48 *oysters, shucked*
- ¾ *teaspoon salt*
- ½ *teaspoon pepper*
- ½ *teaspoon sherry pepper sauce (optional)*
- ½ *teaspoon Tabasco sauce*
- ½ *teaspoon Worcestershire sauce*
- 1½ *quarts (6 cups) heavy cream*
- 5 *red potatoes, cut into 1-inch cubes*
- ¼ *cup (½ stick) butter, cut into pieces*

Heat oil in Dutch oven over high heat until hot. Reduce heat to medium; add oysters, salt, pepper, sherry pepper sauce, Tabasco sauce and Worcestershire sauce. Cook about 3 minutes or until oysters begin to curl around edges. Remove oysters from Dutch oven; set aside.

Add cream to Dutch oven. Simmer over low heat for about 20 minutes or until cream begins to thicken, stirring occasionally.

Meanwhile, cook potatoes in boiling salted water until tender.

Add cooked potatoes and oysters to cream mixture; simmer 1 minute. Remove from heat. Add butter; whisk until melted. Serve immediately.

Broccoli, Crab and Cheddar Quiche

INDIAN PUDDING

Yield: 8 to 12 servings

- ½ *cup brown sugar*
- 3 *teaspoons ginger*
- 3 *teaspoons cinnamon*
- ½ *teaspoon salt*
- 2 *quarts (8 cups) milk*
- ½ *cup (1 stick) butter*
- ¾ *cup cornmeal*
- 1½ *cups molasses*

Heat oven to 350°F. Butter 13x9-inch pan. In large saucepan, combine brown sugar, ginger, cinnamon, salt, milk and butter; mix well. Bring to a boil. Gradually add cornmeal, stirring constantly. Cook until mixture thickens, stirring occasionally. Stir in molasses. Pour mixture into buttered pan.

Bake at 350°F for 1 hour 15 minutes or until pudding is set. Serve warm with vanilla ice cream.

BROCCOLI, CRAB AND CHEDDAR QUICHE

Yield: 6 servings

- 1 *(9-inch) unbaked pie shell*
- 1 *cup chopped fresh broccoli*
- 1 *(4¼-ounce) can crabmeat, drained*
- 1 *cup (4 ounces) shredded mild cheddar cheese*
- 3 *eggs*
- 1 *cup heavy cream*
- ¼ *teaspoon salt*
- ¼ *teaspoon white pepper*

Heat oven to 350°F. Prick unbaked pie shell with fork; bake 7 minutes.

Remove pie shell from oven; place broccoli and crabmeat evenly in bottom of pie shell. Cover broccoli and crabmeat with cheese. In small bowl, beat eggs well; stir in cream, salt and pepper. Pour egg mixture slowly into center of pie shell so mixture spreads evenly.

Bake at 350°F for 35 to 45 minutes or until golden brown. Cut into wedges to serve.

◆ ◆ ◆ ◆ ◆ ◆ ◆ ◆ ◆ ◆

Butter Equivalents:

1 pound	= 4 sticks
	= 2 cups
	= 32 tablespoons
½ pound	= 2 sticks
	= 1 cup
	= 16 tablespoons
¼ pound	= 1 stick
	= ½ cup
	= 8 tablespoons
⅛ pound	= ½ stick
	= ¼ cup
	= 4 tablespoons

◆ ◆ ◆ ◆ ◆ ◆ ◆ ◆ ◆ ◆

Hartness House Inn

Springfield, Vermont

The Hartness House Country Inn is located in Springfield, Vermont.

Built in 1903, the Inn was originally the mansion of James Hartness, astronomer, inventor of the Turret Telescope and Governor of Vermont from 1920-1922.

The Hartness House is rich with history and the staff loves to share it with their guests by providing daily tours of their underground museum. To access the museum, one must travel through a 240 foot tunnel which leads from the main house.

The Inn's "star" attraction... and they mean it literally... is its own telescope, enclosed in an observatory which allows guests to view the moon and stars.

The Hartness House has 40 rooms. The Main House has 11 rooms which are all individually decorated. There are 29 rooms in the connecting annex which are decorated with a country flair. The grounds of the Hartness House consist of colorful and peaceful gardens, an outdoor pool, clay tennis court, and a beautiful 25 acre nature trail.

Dining at the Hartness House is an experience to savor and remember. From intriguing appetizers to tantalizing desserts, everything at the Hartness House is made of the very finest ingredients, expertly prepared and beautifully presented by the Inn's own chef.

Area attractions include the Springfield Art and Historical Center, Eureka Schoolhouse, the oldest remaining schoolhouse in Vermont, and Fort #4, built during the French and Indian War. Golfers can enjoy a fine 18-hole golf course, and the Inn provides self-guided "site and see" tours to many small Vermont towns which include Woodstock and Windsor.

The Hartness House is one of the most unique Country Inns in the United States. Its reputation as a historical place as well as its warm hospitality is known worldwide.

Jalapeño Bread

Yield: 4 loaves

- 1 *package active dry yeast*
- 1 *tablespoon sugar*
- 3 *teaspoons salt*
- 2 *cups warm water (120°F)*
- 5¾ *cups all-purpose flour*
- ¼ *cup chopped fresh or jarred jalapeño chiles*
- ¼ *cup (½ stick) butter, melted*

In large bowl, dissolve yeast, sugar and salt in warm water. Add flour, jalapeño chiles and butter; mix on low speed or with wooden spoon until dough forms.

On floured surface, knead dough for 5 minutes. Place dough in buttered large bowl; cover with towel. Let rise in warm place for 1 hour.

Line with paper or lightly butter 2 cookie sheets, or butter four 8x4-inch loaf pans. When dough has risen, cut into 4 equal portions; roll each into 12-inch loaf. Place 3 inches apart on paper-lined cookie sheets or in loaf pans. Let rise 30 minutes or until doubled in size.

Heat oven to 375°F. Bake 20 to 25 minutes or until light brown.

Apple Normandy Cheesecake

APPLE NORMANDY CHEESECAKE

Yield: 14 to 16 servings

Crust

- 3 *cups graham cracker crumbs*
- ½ *cup (1 stick) butter, melted*

Filling

- 4 *(8-ounce) packages cream cheese, softened*
- 1 *cup sugar*
- 1 *teaspoon vanilla*
- 4 *eggs*
- ¼ *cup all purpose flour*
- 3 *teaspoons cinnamon*
- 2 *tablespoons applejack brandy or*
- ¼ *cup apple juice*
- 14 to 16 *(¼-inch) peeled apple slices*

Heat oven to 325°F. In medium bowl, combine graham cracker crumbs and butter; mix well to moisten. Press crumbs in bottom and 3/4 of the way up sides of 10-inch springform pan. Set aside.

In large bowl, combine cream cheese, sugar and vanilla; mix at medium speed until well mixed. Add eggs one at a time, until of batter consistency. Add flour, cinnamon and brandy or apple juice; gently mix until combined. Pour into crust-lined pan.

Bake at 325°F for 1 hour. Fan apple slices on top of cheesecake; bake an additional 20 to 30 minutes or until center is set. Refrigerate overnight before serving.

HAZELNUT SALMON

Yield: 4 servings

- 4 *(6 to 8-ounce) salmon fillets*
- 1¼ *cups finely chopped hazelnuts*
- 3 to 4 *tablespoons butter*
- ½ *cup water*
- 1 *tablespoon chopped shallots*
- ½ *cup hazelnut liqueur or hazelnut syrup*
- 1 *pint (2 cups) heavy cream*
- ¼ *teaspoon salt*
- ⅛ *teaspoon white pepper*

Heat oven to 350°F. Coat salmon fillets with hazelnuts, pressing in lightly. Melt butter in saute pan or skillet. Brown each salmon fillet about 30 seconds on each side or until light brown. Transfer to 13x9-inch (3-quart) baking dish; add water. Bake at 350°F for 20 to 25 minutes or until salmon is firm to the touch.

To prepare sauce, in small saucepan, combine shallots and liqueur. Cook until reduced by half. Add cream; cook about 15 minutes or until reduced by half, stirring constantly. Continue to cook until sauce begins to thicken. Stir in salt and pepper. To serve, ladle 1/4 cup sauce onto each serving plate; place salmon fillets on sauce. Garnish and serve.

◆ ◆ ◆ ◆ ◆ ◆ ◆ ◆ ◆ ◆

When baking, always check food at the end of the minimum baking time to determine doneness—baking time can vary depending upon the oven.

For best results when baking, bring all ingredients to room temperature.

★

If stored in airtight containers, whole spices and seasonings will keep for one year; ground will keep for six months.

◆ ◆ ◆ ◆ ◆ ◆ ◆ ◆ ◆ ◆

Middle Atlantic

The Middle Atlantic region is nestled between New England and the Southern states. The land in this area varies dramatically, from the rugged Adirondack Mountains in New York to the seemingly endless Atlantic shores of New Jersey and Delaware. To the Native Americans in this region, game was plentiful and many of the same foods consumed by their counterparts in New England were available here, including fish and shellfish. Even great sea turtles were abundant and highly prized for their meat!

Dutch settlers made their mark on the region in the early 1600's. In 1623, they established trading posts in what are now Albany, New York and Camden, New Jersey. And, in what has become the most famous real estate transaction in history, the director of the West India Company purchased the Island of Manhattan in 1624 from the Indians for a value of $25. However, the British became increasingly concerned about the Dutch successes. In 1664, James the Duke of York captured the Dutch Colony of New Netherland, and renamed it New York.

In 1681, William Penn was given a Royal grant for what is now the state of Pennsylvania. Soon thereafter, Penn and his fellow Quakers had settled Philadelphia. German and Dutch refugees (later referred to as Pennsylvania Dutch), hearing about the religious tolerance in this colony, began arriving in 1683 and settled west of Philadelphia. The foods of the Pennsylvania Dutch have since become integral parts of the American food scene and include Sauerbraten, chicken pot pie, corn fritters, dumplings and noodles, and sticky buns.

The Middle Atlantic states are renowned not only for traditional foods, but for special dishes that evolved in their biggest cities. In New York, for example, came Manhattan clam chowder, vichyssoise, eggs Benedict and New York style cheesecake. And the rich ethnic diversity of New York and Philadelphia has added pastrami, Italian cheesesteak sandwiches and Chinese take-out food to the American eating experience.

Beekman 1766 Tavern

Rhinebeck, New York

The Beekman 1766 Tavern is located in the picturesque Hudson Valley, New York town of Rhinebeck.

The Tavern is located in the stately Beekman Arms Hotel. Built in 1766, the hotel was originally known as the Traphagen's Tavern. The American Hotel Association and historians have recognized The Beekman Arms as being the "Oldest Hotel in America" in continuous operation.

Over the years, many other politically famous people have visited the old Inn, as well as many prominent members of the stage and screen.

While staying at the hotel, guests can enjoy delicious meals served at The Beekman 1766 Tavern. The Tavern has been recognized by many food critics and magazines for its outstanding food and service.

The Beekman Arms Hotel was originally a one-story stone building constructed with a dual purpose in mind — to provide bed and board for the weary traveler, and to serve as a shelter for the local residents against Indian attacks. Later, during the Revolutionary War, General Washington often watched his troops drilling in the square from the corner window, while he waited for his couriers to arrive with news of the war.

The town of Rhinebeck offers many unique shops, antique centers and country fairs. Another popular tourist attraction are the tours offered at many of the estates of prominent citizens of America's past.

A trip to the Beekman 1766 Tavern not only guarantees their guests a great meal, but also immerses them in an atmosphere steeped in history.

Fresh Berry Shortcake

Yield: 9 to 12 servings

Shortcakes

- 3½ *cups all-purpose flour*
- ½ *cup sugar*
- 3 *tablespoons baking powder*
- ¾ *cup (1½ sticks) unsalted butter, chilled, cut into pieces*
- 1½ *cups heavy cream*
- 2 to 4 *tablespoons butter, melted*
- 4 to 5 *tablespoons sugar*

Topping

- 4½ to 6 *cups fresh berries (½ cup berries per shortcake)*
- *Sugar to taste*
- 1½ *cups heavy cream*
- 1 *teaspoon vanilla*
- 2 to 3 *tablespoons sugar*

Heat oven to 375°F. Lightly butter cookie sheet. In large bowl, combine flour, 1/2 cup sugar and baking powder. Using fingertips, quickly and lightly work in chilled butter pieces. Add 1 1/2 cups cream; stir just until dough holds together.

Turn dough out onto lightly floured surface; knead dough a few times. Do not overwork dough. Pat or roll dough to a 1/2 to 3/4-inch thickness. Cut into desired shape and size. Brush tops with melted butter; sprinkle with 4 to 5 tablespoons sugar. Place on buttered cookie sheet.

Bake at 375°F for 18 to 22 minutes or until light golden brown.

Meanwhile, clean berries; drain well. Place in bowl; sprinkle with sugar to taste. Whip 1 1/2 cups cream, vanilla and 2-3 tablespoons sugar until soft peaks form.

To serve, gently split baked shortcakes; place on serving plates. Spoon 1/2 cup berries onto bottom half of each shortcake. Top with whipped cream; place top half of shortcakes over cream. Serve immediately.

Chicken Pot Pie with Sweet Potato Biscuit Crust

SWEET POTATO BISCUIT CRUST

Yield: 6 servings

Sweet Potato Biscuit Crust

- 1½ *cups all-purpose flour*
- 2 *teaspoons baking powder*
- 1½ *teaspoons sugar*
- ¼ *teaspoon salt*
- 1 *cup heavy cream*
- ½ *cup mashed cooked sweet potato*
- 2 *teaspoons butter, melted*

Heat oven to 350°F. Butter cookie sheet. In medium bowl, combine flour, baking powder, sugar and salt; mix well. Add cream and sweet potato; mix or knead until dough forms. Turn out onto lightly floured surface; roll or press dough until about 1/2 to 3/4 inch thick and the dimension of top of 2 1/2-quart casserole. Brush with melted butter. Place on buttered cookie sheet. Bake at 350°F for 20 to 25 minutes or until golden brown.

♦ ♦ ♦ ♦ ♦ ♦ ♦ ♦ ♦ ♦

Most fresh herbs will last longer if wrapped in a damp paper towel and stored in the refrigerator. Basil and mint are two exceptions.

♦ ♦ ♦ ♦ ♦ ♦ ♦ ♦ ♦ ♦

CHICKEN POT PIE WITH SWEET POTATO BISCUIT CRUST

Yield: 6 servings

Chicken Pot Pie

- 1 *(4 to 5-pound) roasting chicken, quartered*
- 1½ *quarts (6 cups) chicken broth*
- 1 *carrot, cut up (¾ cup)*
- 1 *stalk celery, cut up (¾ cup)*
- 1 *onion, cut up (¾ cup)*
- 2 *cups mushrooms (domestic and gourmet mixed)*
- 2 *tablespoons unsalted butter*
- 4½ *teaspoons all-purpose flour*
- 2 *tablespoons heavy cream*
- 1 *tablespoon chopped mixed fresh herbs (parsley, sage and thyme)*
- 1 *teaspoon kosher salt*
- ½ *teaspoon fresh cracked black pepper*

Wash chicken; cook chicken in broth until chicken is fork tender and juices run clear, about 1 hour.

Remove chicken from broth; set aside until cool. Skim broth; cook over high heat until about 1 1/2 cups good quality broth remains. Add carrot, celery, onion and mushrooms; simmer until vegetables are crisp-tender. While vegetables are cooking, remove chicken meat in large pieces from bones. Discard any fat or skin.

In another saucepan, melt butter over medium heat. Add flour, stirring constantly with wooden spoon; cook 5 minutes. Whisk into broth and vegetables; bring to a boil, stirring constantly. Reduce heat; simmer 5 minutes.

Add chicken meat to vegetable mixture; stir in cream, herbs, salt and pepper. Simmer an additional 2 to 3 minutes. Spoon hot mixture into 2 1/2-quart casserole; carefully place baked biscuit crust over top.

Bake at 350°F for 12 to 15 minutes. Serve immediately.

♦ ♦ ♦ ♦ ♦ ♦ ♦ ♦ ♦ ♦

When substituting dried herbs for fresh, use one teaspoon dried for each tablespoon fresh.

♦ ♦ ♦ ♦ ♦ ♦ ♦ ♦ ♦ ♦

OLDE MILL INN

Basking Ridge, New Jersey

The Olde Mill Inn is an exquisite Country Inn situated in the beautiful Somerset Hills of Central New Jersey. Located in the town of Basking Ridge, the Inn is in a convenient location for all travel points in the greater New York area. Guests will find the historic charm of the past in surroundings of relaxed luxury with all the conveniences of the present.

The Federalist architecture, dramatic fieldstone entryway, grand piano lounge, opulent drawing room, mahogany paneled lobby and library, and sun drenched breakfast conservatory all contribute to the gracious atmosphere of Olde Mill Inn.

Each of the 102 guest rooms and suites is lavishly furnished and offers a host of modern amenities.

The Grain House Restaurant, adjacent to the Olde Mill Inn, was the original Inn from 1930 to 1977. The building dates back to the eighteenth century and is handsomely trimmed in beamed ceilings, oriental rugs and period antiques. Guests may dine in any of the five dining rooms of the Grain House, each with its own crackling fireplace.

The historic restaurant features American Country Inn fare, fresh "homemade" classics, alfresco dining, a scrumptious Sunday Buffet Brunch, and relaxed pub entertainment.

Guests staying at the Olde Mill Inn can enjoy many of the points of interest in the surrounding area. The U.S. Equestrian Team is located nearby where the top riders in the nation compete in events open to the public. A golfing museum, wild life sanctuary and the Jockey Hollow National Historic Park are just a few of the interesting places a guest may visit in the Basking Ridge area.

The Olde Mill Inn enjoys a deservedly acclaimed reputation for its devotion to its guests, making it one of the most spectacular lodging and dining facilities in New Jersey.

WALNUT CHICKEN WITH MAPLE LEMON BUTTER SAUCE

Yield: 8 servings

16 (3 to 4-ounce) boneless skinless chicken breast halves
½ cup buttermilk
½ cup cornmeal
½ cup ground walnuts
1 teaspoon salt
1 teaspoon dry mustard
1 teaspoon dried tarragon leaves
1 teaspoon black pepper
¼ teaspoon ground red pepper (cayenne)

¼ cup (½ stick) butter
½ cup pure maple syrup
⅓ cup lemon juice (juice of 2 lemons)
1 tablespoon minced shallot
1 tablespoon chopped fresh tarragon
⅛ teaspoon nutmeg
2 cups (4 sticks) butter, chilled, cubed
Salt and pepper to taste

Place chicken breast halves in very large bowl or large baking dish. Add buttermilk; mix gently to coat chicken. Let stand 10 minutes.

Heat oven to 350°F. Lightly butter 2 large shallow baking pans or line with foil. In medium bowl, combine cornmeal, walnuts, salt, mustard, dried tarragon, black pepper and ground red pepper; mix well. Remove chicken from buttermilk; coat all sides of each chicken piece with cornmeal mixture, pressing in firmly so walnuts adhere to chicken.

Melt 1/4 cup butter in large skillet over medium heat. Add chicken; brown lightly on both sides. Place in buttered pans. Bake at 350°F for 25 to 30 minutes or until chicken is fork tender and juices run clear.

Meanwhile, in small saucepan, combine maple syrup, lemon juice, shallot, fresh tarragon and nutmeg; mix well. Cook over medium heat about 15 minutes or until reduced by half. With wire whisk, gradually beat in 1 1/2 cups of the butter. Remove from heat; beat in remaining 1/2 cup butter. Season with salt and pepper.

Pecan Molasses Pork Loin with White Cheddar Mashed Potatoes

Baked Horseradish Salmon with Chardonnay Chive Butter Sauce

Yield: 8 to 12 servings

- *8 to 12 (6 to 8-ounce) salmon filets*
- *1 teaspoon salt*
- *¾ teaspoon pepper*
- *¼ cup Chardonnay (dry white) wine*
- *½ cup prepared horseradish, squeezed to remove excess liquid*
- *¼ cup fresh bread crumbs*
- *1 shallot, minced*

Butter Sauce

- *½ cup Chardonnay (dry white) wine*
- *½ cup heavy cream*
- *3 tablespoons lemon juice*
- *1½ cups (3 sticks) butter, chilled, cubed*
- *1 tablespoon finely chopped fresh parsley*
- *1 tablespoon diagonally sliced fresh chives*

Heat oven to 375°F. Lightly butter shallow baking pan or broiler pan. Arrange salmon filets on buttered pan. Sprinkle with salt and pepper; drizzle with 1/4 cup Chardonnay. In small bowl, combine horseradish, bread crumbs and shallot; mix well. Press into top of each filet.

Bake at 375°F for 12 to 14 minutes or until fish flakes easily with fork.

Meanwhile, in small saucepan, combine 1/2 cup Chardonnay, cream and lemon juice; cook over medium-high heat until reduced to 1/4 cup. With wire whisk, beat in 1 cup of the butter. Remove from heat; beat in remaining 1/2 cup butter until thick and smooth. Stir in parsley and chives. If desired, season with salt and pepper. Serve butter sauce over salmon filets.

Pecan Molasses Pork Loin with White Cheddar Mashed Potatoes

Yield: 8 servings

Pork Loin

- *1 (3-lb.) boneless center-cut pork loin, leaving ¼-inch fat on top, trimmed of remaining fat*
- *1 teaspoon salt*
- *½ teaspoon pepper*
- *½ cup molasses*
- *1 cup chopped pecans*

Sauce

- *4 chipotle chiles*
- *1 teaspoon minced shallot*
- *1 teaspoon minced garlic*
- *4 large oranges (¾ cup zest; 2 cups juice)*
- *1 cup bourbon*
- *¼ cup heavy cream*
- *1¼ cups (2½ sticks) butter, chilled, cut into cubes*

Mashed Potatoes

- *8 medium russet potatoes, peeled, diced (about 10 cups)*
- *1 large garlic clove, sliced*
- *¾ cup (1½ sticks) butter, softened*
- *½ cup (2 ounces) shredded white Cheddar cheese*

Heat oven to 325°F. Line 15x10x1-inch baking pan with foil. Place pork loin, fat side down, in large skillet; cook over medium heat until well browned on all sides. Place in foil-lined pan; sprinkle with salt and pepper. Rub molasses on pork to coat. Sprinkle with pecans. Bake at 325°F for 45 minutes or until thermometer reaches 155°F.

Meanwhile, prepare sauce. In small saucepan, combine chiles, shallot, minced garlic, orange zest, orange juice and bourbon; mix well. Cook over medium heat until almost all liquid has evaporated. Add cream; cook until reduced 3/4. With wire whisk, beat in 3/4 cup of the chilled butter. Remove from heat; beat in remaining 1/2 cup chilled butter. Keep warm.

During last 20 minutes of pork loin roasting time, prepare mashed potatoes. Boil potatoes until dry; do not allow potatoes to get cold. Immediately add 3/4 cup softened butter and the cheese; whip with electric mixer or by hand until smooth.

The Queen Victoria® Inn

Cape May, New Jersey

The Queen Victoria Bed & Breakfast Inn is located in the center of the National Historic Landmark District of Cape May, New Jersey.

Cape May, discovered in 1609 by Sir Henry Hudson, is the nation's first and oldest seashore resort.

The Inn includes three Victorian homes and gardens beautifully restored by Dane and Joan Wells.

All three of the Inn's buildings are painted in the traditional style of the Victorian Era, and landscaped with lovely gardens and trees. One of the main buildings, Prince Albert Hall, features a garden bursting with hundreds upon hundreds of golden daffodils every spring.

All guest rooms at the Queen Victoria are decorated with Victorian antiques, creating a charming informal country Inn atmosphere.

The Queen Victoria Inn and the Queen Cottage serve a full breakfast, afternoon tea, and evening turn down every day of the year. The Inn is known for its festive Christmas decorations and programs. As is their tradition, Dane Wells does his famous tour and discussion every afternoon at 5:00 p.m. for his guests during the holiday season. While viewing and discussing their three nationally known and appropriately decorated trees, guests will learn about the history of the Christmas festival during the Victorian era.

Visitors to Cape May can enjoy many of the historic points of interest in the area. The Emlen Physick Estate is the museum of Victorian living. The Cape May Lighthouse is one of the oldest continually operating lighthouses in America.

The Botanical Gardens offer 27 beautifully designed gardens. Historic Cold Spring Village is a restoration of a South Jersey farm village of the nineteenth century. Historic Weaton Village, an 1881 glass making town, features the Museum of American Glass. There are beautiful inland waterway cruises as well as breathtaking ocean sight-seeing tours around the Cape.

The Queen Victoria Bed and Breakfast Inn proudly offers its guests all the ambiance of the Victorian Era along with the utmost in comfort, service and hospitality.

Lemon Squares

Yield: 48 bars

Base

- 1½ *cups (3 sticks) butter, softened*
- 3 *cups all-purpose flour*
- ¾ *cup powdered sugar*

Topping

- 6 *eggs*
- 3 *cups sugar*
- 1 *tablespoon all-purpose flour*
- 1½ *teaspoons baking powder*
- 3 *tablespoons grated lemon peel*
- 6 *tablespoons lemon juice*
- *Powdered sugar*

Heat oven to 350°F. In large bowl, combine all base ingredients; mix well. Pat evenly in bottom of unbuttered 15x10x1-inch baking pan. Bake at 350°F for 15 minutes.

In same large bowl, combine all topping ingredients; blend well. Pour over baked base.

Bake at 350°F for an additional 20 to 25 minutes or until set. Loosen edges with metal spatula while bars are warm and dust with powdered sugar. Cool completely. Cut into squares.

Koffee Kuchen

KOFFEE KUCHEN

Yield: 8 servings

Kuchen

- *1 cup sugar*
- *½ cup (1 stick) butter*
- *2 eggs, separated*
- *1½ cups all-purpose flour*
- *½ teaspoon baking powder*
- *½ cup milk*

Topping

- *6 tablespoons all-purpose flour*
- *¼ cup firmly packed brown sugar*
- *2 tablespoons butter*
- *½ teaspoon baking powder*

Heat oven to 350°F. Butter 12x8-inch (2-quart) baking dish. In large bowl, beat sugar and 1/2 cup butter until well blended. Add egg yolks; beat well. Sift together 1 1/2 cups flour and 1/2 teaspoon baking powder; add to butter mixture alternately with milk. In small bowl, beat egg whites until stiff; fold gently into batter. Spread batter evenly in buttered dish.

In small bowl, combine all topping ingredients; mix until coarse crumbs form. Sprinkle evenly over batter.

Bake at 350°F for 28 to 32 minutes or until toothpick inserted in center comes out clean. Cut into squares; serve warm.

BAKED PINEAPPLE

Yield: 12 servings

- *1 cup sugar*
- *1 cup (2 sticks) butter, softened*
- *8 eggs, beaten*
- *2 (20-ounce) cans crushed pineapple, drained*
- *12 slices white bread, crusts removed, cubed*

Heat oven to 325°F. Lightly butter a 3-quart glass baking dish. In large bowl, beat sugar and butter until well blended. Add eggs; beat well. Stir in pineapple. Fold in bread cubes. Pour into buttered dish.

Bake at 325°F for 45 to 50 minutes or until bubbly and knife inserted in center comes out clean.

Recipe can be prepared in advance, covered and refrigerated. If baked directly from refrigerator, uncover and bake at 325°F for 55 to 60 minutes. For variety, add cubed ham or sprinkle top with crumbled bacon.

♦ ♦ ♦ ♦ ♦ ♦ ♦ ♦ ♦ ♦

Butter Curls

Use a 1/4-pound stick of butter that has been kept at room temperature for several minutes until it softens slightly but is still firm. Heat butter curler in very hot water, then pull lightly but firmly over the butter to form curls. If curls break, the butter is too cold. Reheat curler as necessary.

♦ ♦ ♦ ♦ ♦ ♦ ♦ ♦ ♦ ♦

Asa Ransom House

Clarence, New York

Asa Ransom House is located in the town of Clarence, New York. The interesting history of the Inn began in the late 1700's.

In 1799, the Holland Land Company offered land in what is now the town of Clarence, to "any poor man who would build and operate a tavern on it." The first to accept this offer was a young silversmith by the name of Asa Ransom, who had been plying his trade in the little fur trading post on the shores of Lake Erie.

In the hollow of the ledge near a pine grove, Mr. Ransom built a combination log cabin home and tavern. In 1801, Asa Ransom built a sawmill near the creek that bears his name, and in 1803 he built a grist mill, the first in what is now Erie County.

The original building, housing the library, gift shop and tap room dates back to 1853 and perhaps earlier. The brick wall in the hall was the outside of the original building. The dining rooms were added in 1975 with careful concern to keep the charm of the 19th century. The ruins of the grist mill are at the rear of the Inn property.

The charm of the past and the convenience of the present have been brought together in the picturesque rooms. Each bedroom is furnished with antiques and period reproductions, offered at the Inn.

The menu reflects a real New York farmland feeling. A cheery fire warms you in the winter, and the many windows overlooking the garden and lawn charm you in the summer. Many of the herbs used in the kitchen are grown in their herb and flower garden. Its two dining rooms contrast each other with the Ransom Room being Country formal and the Clarence Hollow being Country rustic.

Clarence, New York abounds with antique shops, many within walking distance of the Inn. The Town Park, just a few steps away, offers shaded lawns, a duck pond, and outdoor summer twilight concerts. Here, tennis and swimming are also available to their guests. The Clarence Center Emporium and Ice Cream Parlor (historic restoration) are just a short distance away.

The history and ambiance of the Asa Ransom House combined with the impeccable service and food, guarantees its guests a truly memorable stay.

Cinnamon Swirl Breakfast Cake

Yield: 12 servings

- ¾ *cup (1½ sticks) butter, melted, cooled*
- 1 *cup sugar*
- 3 *eggs*
- 3 *cups all-purpose flour*
- 3 *teaspoons baking powder*
- 1½ *cups milk*
- 1 *teaspoon vanilla*
- 1½ *cups sugar*
- 3 *teaspoons cinnamon*

Heat oven to 350°F. Generously butter 13x9-inch pan. In large bowl, combine cooled melted butter, 1 cup sugar and eggs; beat well. Add flour, baking powder, milk and vanilla; mix well. Pour into buttered pan.

In small bowl, combine 1 1/2 cups sugar and cinnamon; mix well. Sprinkle over batter; with spoon, marble into batter.

Bake at 350°F for 35 to 45 minutes or until toothpick inserted in center comes out clean. If desired, brush top of warm cake with additional butter. If desired, when cool, sprinkle with powdered sugar.

Butter Pecan Pastry

Butter Pecan Pastry

Yield: 12 to 16 servings

__*Pastry*__

- *1½ cups (3 sticks) butter (salted)*
- *4 cups all-purpose flour*
- *1 cup ground pecans*
- *⅔ cup cold water*
- *1 egg, beaten*

__*Filling*__

- *½ cup (1 stick) butter*
- *½ cup sugar*
- *¼ cup all-purpose flour*
- *1 cup ground pecans*

To make pastry, in large bowl, combine all pastry ingredients except water and egg; blend well. Add water; mix well. Refrigerate 2 to 3 hours or overnight.

Heat oven to 375°F. Butter cookie sheet or pizza pan. To make filling, in another large bowl, beat 1/2 cup butter and sugar until well blended. Add 1/4 cup flour and 1 cup pecans; blend well.

Divide dough into 2 portions; roll out 1 portion into 10-inch circle. Place on buttered cookie sheet. Spread filling to 1 inch from edge. Roll out remaining portion of dough into 10-inch circle; brush edge with water. Place pastry on top of filling; press and crimp edge. Brush top with beaten egg.

Bake 375°F for 35 to 40 minutes or until golden brown. Cut into wedges to serve. Serve with dollop of Rum Flavored Hard Sauce.

Rum Flavored Hard Sauce for Butter Pecan Pastry

Yield: 1½ cups

- *½ cup (1 stick) butter, softened*
- *1 cup powdered sugar*
- *½ teaspoon rum, or*
- *½ teaspoon rum flavoring*

In small bowl, combine ingredients; beat well. Serve dollop on each serving of Butter Pecan Pastry.

Brownie Mania

Yield: 24 to 36 bars

- *1 cup (2 sticks) butter, melted, cooled*
- *2 cups sugar*
- *6 eggs*
- *1 cup unsweetened cocoa*
- *½ cup all-purpose flour*
- *2 teaspoons baking powder*
- *2 teaspoons vanilla*
- *½ cup chopped pecans*
- *½ cup white chips*
- *½ cup butterscotch chips*
- *½ cup semi-sweet chocolate chips*

Heat oven to 350°F. Butter 13x9-inch pan. In large bowl, combine cooled butter, sugar and eggs; beat well. Add cocoa, flour, baking powder and vanilla; mix well. Stir in pecans and all chips. Spread in buttered pan.

Bake at 350°F for 40 to 50 minutes or until center is set. Cool completely. Cut into squares.

THE SOUTH

The South is rich in color, history and pride. From its gardens come colorful dogwoods and azaleas, and fragrant gardenias and magnolias. From its fields and towns have come some of the nation's most important historical events. And from the kitchens of tidewater Maryland to the bayous of Louisiana have come some of the country's finest regional dishes.

Bordered on the east by the Atlantic and the south by the Gulf of Mexico, the South has a temperate climate that greatly contributes to its diverse cuisine. This environment is ideal for such crops as citrus, corn, and peanuts, while its waters produce an abundance of oysters, crabs, shrimp, crayfish, trout and catfish.

The region's cuisine is also very much a product of its history. The south by the gulf, like New England, was founded by English immigrants. Here, colonists were also greatly aided by Native Americans, who taught them how and what to farm. The first settlers in Jamestown, Virginia, quickly learned about maize, or corn, from the local Powhatan Algonquian tribes. The colonists had also been fortunate enough to bring along pigs, which thrived in the new environment. Within a few months, the basis of Southern cooking had been established. Corn and pork are still the foundation of the Southern kitchen today.

Later, the region's food was influenced by other distinct immigrant groups. Africans brought a new dimension to the traditional soups, stews and vegetables of plantation kitchens with the use of herbs, spices and tomatoes. Years later, the French introduced new flavors along the coastal areas from Charleston to New Orleans, while the Spanish inspired the unique flavors of Florida. The distinctive Creole and Cajun cuisines of New Orleans, which have lately become some of the most popular styles of Southern cooking, evolved from a combination of the classic French cuisine and the many spicy ingredients used in Spanish country cooking.

From a graceful plantation to simple country homes, Southerners have long been known for their gracious hospitality. When people get together, they usually do so over good food. The traditional Southern recipes handed down among generations include rich buttery pecan pie, key lime pie, peach pie, corn and rice pudding, buttermilk biscuits, coconut cake, banana foster, grits and savory gumbos and jambalayas.

Clifton — The Country Inn

Charlottesville, Virginia

Clifton — The Country Inn is located in the historic town of Charlottesville, Virginia. Situated in the rolling hills and picturesque valleys of Albemarle County, the tranquil surroundings are a perfect setting for a Country Inn.

The Inn was built in 1799 and is believed to have been built as an office. It then became the residence of the elderly Thomas Mann Randolph, who served as Governor of Virginia, a member of the U.S. Congress, and was the husband to Thomas Jefferson's beloved daughter, Martha.

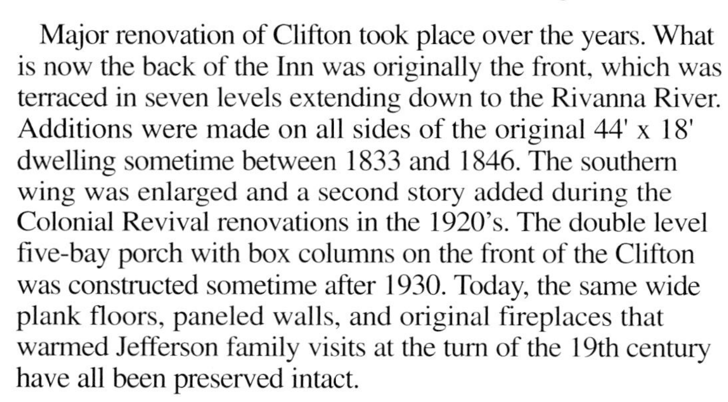

Major renovation of Clifton took place over the years. What is now the back of the Inn was originally the front, which was terraced in seven levels extending down to the Rivanna River. Additions were made on all sides of the original 44' x 18' dwelling sometime between 1833 and 1846. The southern wing was enlarged and a second story added during the Colonial Revival renovations in the 1920's. The double level five-bay porch with box columns on the front of the Clifton was constructed sometime after 1930. Today, the same wide plank floors, paneled walls, and original fireplaces that warmed Jefferson family visits at the turn of the 19th century have all been preserved intact.

The Clifton Inn offers fourteen beautifully appointed rooms and suites, each featuring a fireplace, antique or canopy bed, and French windows with summer views of the lake and winter views of Jefferson's Monticello. Guests may dine in an elegant dining room and relax in the gracious drawing room, library and garden room.

Recreational amenities include a spectacular pool with waterfall, year-round heated spa, croquet, clay tennis court, and a secluded lake for fishing, swimming and tubing — all surrounded by forty acres of woods and trails.

The Clifton is known for its universal cuisine prepared by its award winning chef, Craig Hartman. Breakfast is served in the Clifton's paneled dining room, or on the veranda. During the week, five course gourmet dinners are offered, and on Friday and Saturday six course dinners are served with pre-dinner entertainment.

There is much to see and do within a short distance of the Inn. Guests can visit Jefferson's Monticello, James Monroe's Estate, Ash Lawn, and the historic Michie Tavern. Downtown Charlottesville has a distinctly European feeling, with its pedestrian-friendly street of shops and outdoor cafés.

As a guest of Clifton — The Country Inn, you will experience first-hand the beauty, splendor and graciousness of true Southern hospitality.

Essence of Asparagus Soup

Yield: 10 (1½-cup) servings

- ½ *cup (1 stick) butter*
- 2 *large onions, diced (2 cups)*
- 2 *pounds asparagus, thinly sliced*
- ½ *cup chopped fresh chives*
- ½ *teaspoon sugar*
- ½ *teaspoon salt*
- ¼ *teaspoon pepper*
- 2 *quarts (8 cups) vegetarian vegetable bouillon*
- ¼ *cup water*
- 4 *tablespoons cornstarch*
- 1 *cup heavy cream*

In Dutch oven or large saucepan, melt butter over medium-high heat. Add onions; cook about 5 to 10 minutes, stirring frequently. Add asparagus, chives, sugar, salt and pepper; cook an additional 4 minutes, stirring frequently.

Reduce heat to medium-low; cover and cook for 5 to 10 minutes. Add bouillon; cover and simmer for 20 minutes.

In small bowl, combine water and cornstarch; blend well. Stir cornstarch mixture into soup. Return to a boil; simmer 5 minutes. Remove from heat; stir in cream. Serve immediately.

Chocolate-Chambord Bavarian Cream

CLIFTON'S CRAB AND CORN CHOWDER

Yield: 12 (1 ½-cup) servings

- ½ *pound bacon, diced*
- ½ *cup (1 stick) butter*
- 2 *medium onions, diced*
- 4 *stalks celery, diced*
- 6 *medium potatoes, diced*
- ½ *cup all-purpose flour*
- 1½ *quarts (6 cups) reduced-sodium chicken or vegetable broth*
- 2 *(15-ounce) cans cream style corn*
- 3 *cups fresh or frozen corn*
- ¼ *cup chopped fresh parsley*
- ¼ *cup chopped fresh chives*
- 1 *pint (2 cups) heavy cream*
- 1 *pound lump or 3 (6-ounce) cans crabmeat, drained*

In large skillet, cook bacon over medium heat until soft but not crisp. Add butter; melt. Add onions and celery; cook until partially cooked. Add potatoes; cook, stirring frequently, until vegetables are tender. Stir in flour; cook, stirring constantly, for 5 minutes.

Stir in broth until smooth. Reduce heat; simmer 20 to 30 minutes, stirring occasionally to prevent sticking.

Stir in cream style and whole kernel corn, parsley, chives, salt and pepper. Bring just to a boil. Gently stir in cream and crabmeat; cook just until heated. Serve immediately.

CHOCOLATE-CHAMBORD BAVARIAN CREAM

Yield: 8 servings

- 1 *envelope unflavored gelatin*
- 2 *tablespoons cold water*
- 1 *cup half-and-half*
- ½ *vanilla bean*
- ¼ *cup sugar*
- 1 *teaspoon Chambord (raspberry-flavored) liqueur*
- 1 *egg yolk*
- 4 *ounces semi-sweet chocolate, melted*
- 1½ *cups heavy cream, whipped*

In small bowl, sprinkle gelatin over cold water; set aside. In small saucepan, heat half-and-half and vanilla bean until very warm but not boiling. Remove vanilla bean; discard.

Pour half-and-half mixture into another small bowl. Add sugar, liqueur and egg yolk; mix well with wire whisk. Return mixture to saucepan; cook over low heat for about 15 minutes or until mixture coats back of spoon, stirring occasionally.

Remove saucepan from heat. With wire whisk, stir gelatin mixture into hot mixture until dissolved. Add melted chocolate; stir until smooth and well combined. Cool 1 hour at room temperature.

Fold whipped cream into mixture. Spoon into 8 individual molds. Refrigerate 4 hours or until firm.

To serve, if desired, drizzle 1 tablespoon Chambord liqueur onto each dessert plate. Unmold desserts onto plates. If desired, garnish each serving with fresh raspberries and mint leaves.

◆ ◆ ◆ ◆ ◆ ◆ ◆ ◆ ◆ ◆

Store potatoes in a well ventilated, dark, dry area.

★

Do not break apart celery stalks until you are ready to use them or they will wilt quickly.

★

Celery wrapped in plastic will keep up to two weeks in refrigerator.

★

A partially frozen onion is easier to slice and chop and won't irritate your eyes.

◆ ◆ ◆ ◆ ◆ ◆ ◆ ◆ ◆ ◆

Opryland Hotel

Nashville, Tennessee

The Opryland Hotel is located in the country music capital of the United States — Nashville, Tennessee. Opened in 1977, the hotel is a blend of Colonial Williamsburg and Southern Plantation architectural styles. As part of Opryland USA, it is one of the largest and most distinctive resorts in the nation.

Opryland USA is an entertainment resort that includes the Opryland Themepark, the Grand Ole Opry, and cable television's The Nashville Network and Country Music Television.

Highlights of Opryland Hotel are the Cascades Conservatory and the Delta. The Cascades Conservatory consists of two gardens under glass accented by skylights that connect six-story wings of guest rooms. The Delta, opened in June 1996, is a 4.5 acre interiorscope featuring shops, restaurants, and a river with flatboats. The hotel has 2,883 rooms, many of which overlook the three spectacular indoor gardens.

A variety of dining opportunities complement Opryland Hotel's entertainment. The Old South is recalled at Rhett's, a restaurant serving American regional favorites and at Beauregards in the Delta offering cuisine with a New Orleans flair. The Cascades Restaurant and The Old Hickory Steakhouse offer Continental menus. Other choices are Rachel's Kitchen, the Delta Food Court, The Veranda and more. Whether casual or elegant, all of the restaurants are overseen by an award-winning culinary staff.

Nashville offers visitors an array of exciting and fun points of interest from the Wildhorse Saloon, Ryman Auditorium and Country Music Hall of Fame in downtown Nashville to historic sites like the Parthenon, and The Hermitage, home of President Andrew Jackson.

There is no place quite like Opryland Hotel. Its tradition of comfort and space, and its panorama of tastes and styles are all presented with the courtesy that is the standard of the South.

Italian Cheese Mold

Yield: 4 servings

- 2¼ *cups (8 ounces) freshly grated Parmesan cheese*
- ¼ *cup virgin olive oil*
- ½ *cup all-purpose flour*
- 2⅓ *cups warm milk*
- 3 *eggs*
- 2 *tablespoons butter*
- ⅛ *teaspoon nutmeg*
- ½ *teaspoon salt*
- ¼ *teaspoon pepper*

Heat oven to 350°F. Butter 5-cup mold; sprinkle evenly with 2 tablespoons of the cheese.

In medium saucepan, heat oil over medium heat until warm. Add flour; cook, stirring constantly, about 2 minutes or until oil has soaked up all of the flour. While stirring constantly, gradually add milk; cook 5 to 8 minutes or until thickened and smooth. Remove from heat; cool to room temperature.

Add eggs one at a time, beating well after each addition. Stir in remaining cheese, nutmeg, salt and pepper until well blended. Pour into cheese-coated mold; place mold in baking dish half-filled with water.

Bake at 350°F for 60 to 70 minutes or until deep golden brown and knife inserted in center comes out clean. Cool in mold 15 minutes. Loosen edges with knife; remove from mold. Serve with your favorite zesty tomato sauce.

Oriental Chicken Quiche

ORIENTAL CHICKEN QUICHE

Yield: 6 servings

- *3 tablespoons butter*
- *½ pound boneless skinless chicken breast halves, cut into ½-inch pieces*
- *8 pea pods, cut in strips*
- *2 green onions, sliced*
- *½ red bell pepper, seeded, diced*
- *1 to 2 tablespoons soy sauce*
- *1 tablespoon grated gingerroot*
- *⅛ teaspoon ground red pepper (cayenne)*
- *1 (9-inch) unbaked pie shell*
- *3 eggs*
- *1 cup (4 ounce) shredded Swiss cheese*
- *¼ teaspoon salt, if desired*
- *⅛ teaspoon pepper*
- *⅛ teaspoon nutmeg*
- *1 tablespoon heavy cream*
- *Dash Worcestershire sauce*

Heat oven to 350°F. Melt butter in large skillet. Add chicken, peas, onions and bell pepper; cook and stir 6 to 8 minutes or until chicken is no longer pink. Stir in soy sauce, gingerroot and ground red pepper. Spread mixture in unbaked pie shell.

In medium bowl, beat eggs well. Add cheese, salt, pepper, nutmeg, cream and Worcestershire sauce; mix well. Pour over chicken and vegetables in pie shell.

Bake at 350°F for 45 to 50 minutes or until golden brown and filling is firm. Cut into wedges to serve.

CREAM CHEESE AND ROASTED PEPPER DIP

Yield: 1 cup

- *1 green bell pepper*
- *½ cup sour cream*
- *¼ cup cream cheese*
- *¼ teaspoon Worcestershire sauce*
- *¼ cup chopped onion*
- *1 garlic clove, chopped*
- *Salt and hot pepper sauce to taste*
- *1 tablespoon finely chopped chives*

Broil bell pepper 4 to 6 inches from heat, turning often, until skin has blackened. Place blackened bell pepper in small bowl; cover tightly with plastic wrap. Cool. Peel bell pepper; cut in half. Remove stem, inner membranes and seeds; discard. Dice bell pepper; set aside.

Combine sour cream, cream cheese, Worcestershire sauce, onion, and garlic in food processor bowl with metal blade; cover and process until smooth. Season with salt and hot pepper sauce. Transfer mixture to mixing bowl; stir in bell pepper and chives. Cover; refrigerate. Serve as a dip with raw vegetables.

♦ ♦ ♦ ♦ ♦ ♦ ♦ ♦ ♦ ♦

For maximum flavor, heat butter before using. Heating releases natural flavor compounds, allowing butter to develop its full, rich taste. Drizzle over vegetables, pasta and grains, potatoes or broiled fish and poultry.

♦ ♦ ♦ ♦ ♦ ♦ ♦ ♦ ♦ ♦

Camberley's MARTHA WASHINGTON INN

Abingdon, Virginia

Camberley's Martha Washington Inn is nestled in the Blue Ridge Highlands, one of Southwest Virginia's most cherished areas. Located in the town of Abingdon, the Inn was built in 1832 as the private home of Brigadier General and Mrs. Francis Preston and their nine children. The house was decorated with many priceless furnishings. Over the years many of Virginia's famous and powerful passed through the doors of the Preston home. General Preston died in 1835 and his wife sold the mansion in 1858. The mansion was soon to become a prominent college for young women known as the Martha Washington College. Unfortunately, the devastating Civil War was soon to have a dramatic effect on the college. Schoolgirls became nurses, and the beautiful grounds became training barracks for the Washington Mounted Rifles. Despite the war, the college survived, but the Great Depression and the declining enrollment eventually took its toll. The College closed its doors in 1932, standing idle for several years.

Around 1935, the building was opened as a true hotel and through the years saw many renovations. Fortunately, much of the Inn's historic charm, antiques, and architectural details were preserved. In 1984, the Inn was purchased by The United Company and underwent an eight million dollar renovation. Sensitive to the building's enduring historic legacy, the restoration preserved and enhanced much of its original charm and architectural detail. In 1995, the Inn was acquired by the Camberley Hotel Company.

Camberley's Martha Washington Inn has 61 elegantly appointed guest rooms, many of them decorated with beautiful antique beds and furnishings.

Abingdon has numerous seasonal festivals including a Christmas candlelight tour of historic homes, the Virginia Highlands Festival and the Washington County Fair. The area also provides a 34 mile scenic railroad bed converted into a recreational facility for hikers, bikers, joggers, nature walkers, cross-country skiers and equestrians. Guests may also find many shops with handmade crafts, pottery and antiques.

Camberley's Martha Washington Inn is presently rated as a four-star hotel, and is dedicated to seeing that each guest is treated in the true tradition of this region.

RICOTTA CHEESECAKE

Yield: 8 to 10 servings

Crust

- 2 teaspoons butter, softened
- ¼ cup crushed graham crackers

Filling

- 3 eggs
- 1½ pounds (3 cups) Ricotta cheese
- ⅔ cup sugar
- ⅓ cup sour cream
- ⅓ cup cornstarch
- 1 teaspoon baking powder
- 3 tablespoons butter, melted, cooled
- 2 teaspoons grated lemon peel
- 1 teaspoon vanilla
- 2 cups cut-up fresh fruit

Heat oven to 325°F. Spread 2 teaspoons butter over bottom and sides of 9-inch springform pan with removable bottom; sprinkle with graham cracker crumbs. Set aside.

In blender or large bowl of electric mixer, combine eggs, Ricotta cheese, sugar and sour cream; blend or beat until smooth. In small bowl, combine cornstarch and baking powder. Add to cheese mixture with 3 tablespoons butter, lemon peel and vanilla; beat well. Pour into crumb-coated pan.

Bake at 325°F for 55 to 60 minutes or until knife inserted in center comes out clean. Cool on wire rack. Cover; refrigerate until cold. To serve, remove sides of pan; cut into wedges and serve with fresh fruit.

Wonton Cinnamon Crisps

WONTON CINNAMON CRISPS

Yield: 40 crisps

- *3 to 4 tablespoons butter, melted*
- *20 wonton skins*
- *¼ cup sugar*
- *1 tablespoon cinnamon*

Heat oven to 375°F. Brush some of butter over bottom of 15x10x1-inch baking pan. Cut each wonton skin in half to make 2 rectangles. Arrange skins (as many as will fit in single layer) side by side in buttered pan. Brush tops with butter. In small bowl, combine sugar and cinnamon; mix well. Sprinkle evenly over skins.

Bake at 375°F for 5 to 7 minutes until crisp and golden brown. Remove crisps from pan; cool on wire racks. Repeat with remaining skins. Serve alone or with your favorite ice cream.

FLAVORED BUTTERS

Chive Butter:

- *1 pound (4 sticks) salted butter, softened*
- *1 bunch chopped chives (¼ cup)*

Garlic Butter:

- *1 pound (4 sticks) salted butter, softened*
- *2 garlic cloves, pureed*

In medium bowl, combine butter and chives or garlic; blend well. Cover; store in refrigerator.

◆ ◆ ◆ ◆ ◆ ◆ ◆ ◆ ◆ ◆

To cream butter, use softened butter or cut refrigerated butter into squares, then beat with electric mixer until light and fluffy.

◆ ◆ ◆ ◆ ◆ ◆ ◆ ◆ ◆ ◆

Butter Varieties

Lightly Salted Butter — Lightly salted butter is used as table butter and for general cooking. When creating flavored butters, lightly salted butter is best used in savory butters, such as those containing herbs or wine.

Unsalted Butter — Unsalted butter, also known as "sweet butter," has no salt added and has the rich, pure taste of sweet cream. Best used for baking or when making sweet flavored butters.

Whipped Butter — Whipped butter contains more air and moisture than regular butter. It spreads more easily when chilled than regular butter, and is generally used as a table spread. Because its weight and density is not the same as an equal measure of regular butter, it should not be used in recipes unless specified.

Cultured Butter — Cultured butter, found more frequently in Europe than in the U.S., is made with cream, to which active cultures have been added. This produces a distinctive, pleasingly tangy flavored butter with a somewhat shorter shelf life.

THE WEST

The discovery and settlement of the American West is the stuff of myths, legends and Hollywood movies. But it also provides the script for one of the most important chapters in American history, and in the development of our uniquely American cuisine. From the endless beaches of Southern California to the rugged coast of the Pacific Northwest, the region boasts some of the country's most breathtaking sights and its most "modern" cooking.

When one thinks about the West and its storied past, images of California and the Gold Rush first come to mind. Set apart from settlements along the Atlantic by the vast continent, California was the most isolated place in America. Geography encouraged the first settlers to use whatever was at their disposal to develop the basis of a local cuisine, thereby instilling an independent, adventurous spirit in food preparation. After the Gold Rush of the mid-1800's, a mix of cultural influences gave California cooking more depth and complexity. Spanish missionaries introduced olives, figs, almonds, dates, chilies, peaches, plums and nectarines. The padres also raised cattle, hogs, and sheep and planted the first vineyards in the region. Later, Mexican ranchers added Southwestern spices, while Europeans and Asians, attracted by the prospect of "gold in the hills," brought their native foods: artichokes, eggplant, broccoli, French prunes and Chinese vegetables. Today, Californians enjoy a cuisine that is casual, light and centered on fresh foods.

Not to be outdone, the Pacific Northwest — Oregon and Washington — offers its own generous culinary landscape along with its rich history. From crystal rivers splashing with salmon and silver fish to endless green forests populated with game and mushrooms, the region boasts some of the country's greatest natural — and food — resources. No one ethnic tradition dominates the culinary style of the Northwest. At the turn of the nineteenth century, Spanish and English attempts at settlements in the area failed. The first successful immigrant communities were established in the 1840's when wagon trains arrived from Missouri. Encouraged by reports from explorers Lewis and Clark, German, Scandinavian and Basque pioneers pursued the Oregon Trail in search of an abundance of natural resources. It didn't take long for them to capitalize on their newfound bounty. Scandinavian dairy farmers raised cows that produced large amounts of pure milk, and Northwestern cheesemakers have earned a national reputation for Oregon Blue and Tillamook Cheddar. Contemporary food from the Northwest tends toward light, fresh and healthful fare - and that's what you'd expect from the home of apples, pears, salmon and Dungeness crabs.

CARTER HOUSE

Eureka, California

The Carter House is located 75 miles south of the Oregon border in the historic 19th century seaport town of Eureka, California.

The Carter House is an enclave of three magnificent Victorian structures perched alongside Humboldt Bay.

The owners of the Carter House, Mark and Christi Carter, purchased a small home in Eureka in 1977 with the intentions of not only living in their new home, but also to rent out a couple of the rooms to guests. Soon the Carters realized how much they enjoyed being innkeepers and decided to build their own 1890 San Francisco style Victorian Inn. It took two years to complete and the results were spectacular. Mark and Christi filled the four story structure with beautiful antiques, oriental carpets, paintings by local artists, and lots of fresh flowers.

With the tremendous success of the Carter House, the Carters built the Hotel Carter across the street. The twenty guestrooms are graciously decorated with antiques, beautiful carved headboards and lush down comforters. Many of the rooms have fireplaces and windows with stunning views of the bay.

Dining at the Hotel Carter is a true culinary experience. Guests dine overlooking the bay while enjoying a fabulous breakfast of specially roasted coffee, freshly squeezed orange juice, homemade quiches, pastries and eggs Benedict. Dinners showcase the herbs, greens and vegetables grown in their own organic gardens, as well as the finest seasonal delicacies. The Carter House culinary credentials include membership in New York City's prestigious James Beard Foundation, and many feature articles in culinary magazines.

Steeped in history, Eureka offers visitors numerous museums, art galleries, boutiques, antique shops and theaters. The town boasts more than 1,500 structures of historical importance and has been called the "Williamsburg of the West." Ancient forests of giant redwoods at the Redwood National Park as well as the beautiful beaches are also popular tourist destinations.

Staying at the Carter House is much more than just opulent surroundings and luxurious comforts; it's about good friends, beautiful food and the natural gifts of each season which give our lives a very special grace and magic.

FRESH PACIFIC SALMON ROSEMARY-MUSTARD SAUCE

Yield: 4 servings

2 to 4 tablespoons butter
2 to 4 tablespoons extra-virgin olive oil
4 (6½ to 7-ounce) salmon fillets
½ teaspoon salt
¼ teaspoon white pepper
1 cup white wine
2 tablespoons chopped shallots
4 sprigs fresh rosemary, coarsely chopped
1 tablespoon Dijon mustard
½ cup heavy cream
Fresh rosemary sprigs for garnish

Heat oil and butter in large skillet until butter is melted. Sprinkle salmon fillets with salt and pepper. Cook salmon until golden. Remove salmon from skillet; keep warm.

In same skillet, combine shallots, chopped fresh rosemary, mustard, wine and cream. Cook, stirring occasionally, until sauce is thickened and reduced by 1/2. Place salmon fillets on serving plates; finish with mustard sauce. Garnish each serving with rosemary sprig.

Stuffed Summer Squash

STUFFED SUMMER SQUASH

Yield: 6 servings

- 6 *small whole summer squash*
- 3 *tablespoons extra-virgin olive oil*
- *Dash salt and pepper*
- 1 *teaspoon minced garlic*
- 1 *pound new potatoes*
- 3 *tablespoons unsalted butter, melted*
- ½ *cup heavy cream*
- ½ *cup finely chopped yellow onion*
- 3 *cups chopped summer squash*
- 2 *tablespoons minced fresh parsley*
- 1 *tablespoon minced fresh chives*
- 1 *teaspoon minced fresh sage*
- 1 *teaspoon minced fresh thyme*
- ½ *teaspoon salt*
- ¼ *teaspoon pepper*
- *Fresh herb sprigs and 1 seeded, diced, fresh tomato for garnish*

Heat oven to 325°F. Cut off and reserve tops of whole squash. With spoon, scoop out squash pulp; reserve pulp. Rub all sides of squash shells and tops with 1 tablespoon of the oil. Sprinkle with dash salt and pepper. Place 1/2 teaspoon of the garlic in shells; place shells and tops in 13x9-inch (3-quart) baking dish. Cover dish with foil.

Bake at 325°F for 25 to 30 minutes or until squash are tender but still hold their shape.

Meanwhile, boil potatoes in salted water until tender. Drain potatoes; place in food processor bowl with metal blade. Add butter and cream; process until potatoes are coarsely chopped.

In large skillet, heat remaining 2 tablespoons olive oil over medium-high heat until hot. Add onion and remaining 1/2 teaspoon garlic; cook and stir about 5 minutes. Add reserved squash pulp and chopped squash; cook an additional 10 minutes or until squash is very tender, stirring occasionally.

Add potato mixture, parsley, chives, sage, thyme, salt and pepper; blend well. Stuff squash shells with warm squash filling. Garnish with herb sprigs and diced tomato. Serve immediately.

MEXICAN TOASTED ALMOND COOKIES

Yield: 3½ dozen cookies

- 2 *cups all-purpose flour*
- 1 *cup slivered almonds, toasted*
- ¾ *cup powdered sugar*
- ¼ *teaspoon salt*
- ¼ *teaspoon cinnamon*
- 1 *teaspoon almond extract*
- 1 *cup (2 sticks) butter, softened*
- 1½ *teaspoons grated lemon peel*
- 1½ *teaspoons grated orange peel*

Heat oven to 350°F. Lightly butter cookie sheet. In food processor, combine flour, almonds, 1/2 cup of the powdered sugar, salt and cinnamon; process until mixed. Stir in almond extract, lemon peel and orange peel. Gradually add butter, processing until ball forms. Shape dough into 3/4 to 1-inch balls; place on buttered cookie sheet. Flatten slightly to form small patties.

Bake at 350°F for 12 to 15 minutes or until cookies are very light brown. Remove cookies from cookie sheet; cool on wire racks. Dust cooled cookies with remaining 1/4 cup powdered sugar.

THE MARTINE INN

Pacific Grove, California

The Martine Inn sits high on the cliffs of Pacific Grove overlooking the rocky coastline of the Monterey Bay. The original Victorian building was built in 1899. In 1901, James and Laura Parke of Parke-Davis Pharmaceuticals purchased it for their family. The house was originally a true Victorian, but through the years the Parke's transformed it into a gracious Mediterranean style house using many exotic and unusual woods, such as Siamese Teak, Honduras Mahogany and Spanish Cedar.

In 1942, the Parke's sold their estate to Nancy Ryan who, after thirty years sold it to Homer and Nora Martine and their son, Don. In the early eighties following their marriage, Don and Marion Martine completely renovated the Inn. After the completion of the building restoration, Don and Marion researched authentic Victorian wallcoverings and paint colors to complete the luxurious interior design.

Each of the rooms, some with spectacular water views, are beautifully decorated with furnishings that have been carefully selected to fit the style and ambiance of that room.

A full breakfast is served in the true Victorian style of silver, fine china, crystal and lace.

While visiting the Martine Inn, guests may enjoy many of the interesting sights and events of the surrounding areas. Monterey and Carmel offer aquariums, tours of historic buildings as well as the Monterey Jazz Festival.

Pacific Grove is also host to many festivals throughout the year. One of the most popular is the Butterfly Festival in late September, with the arrival of millions of migrating Monarch butterflies. The town celebrates with a butterfly parade and festivities.

The Martine's attention to detail and gracious hospitality has enabled the Inn to be recognized as one of the best and most romantic bed and breakfasts in the United States.

AGNES' ZUCCHINI COOKIES

Yield: 4 dozen cookies

- 1 *cup sugar*
- ½ *cup (1 stick) unsalted butter, softened*
- 1 *egg, beaten*
- 1 *cup grated zucchini or yellow summer squash*
- 2 *cups all-purpose flour*
- 1 *teaspoon baking soda*
- 1 *teaspoon cinnamon*
- ½ *teaspoon salt*
- ½ *teaspoon cloves*
- 1 *cup raisins*
- 1 *cup chopped walnuts*

Heat oven to 375°F. Butter cookie sheets. In large bowl, combine sugar and butter; beat with electric mixer until light and fluffy. Add egg; beat well. Stir in zucchini or yellow summer squash. In medium bowl, combine flour, baking soda, cinnamon, salt and cloves; mix well. Add to butter mixture; blend well. Stir in raisins and walnuts. Drop by rounded teaspoons 2 inches apart onto buttered cookie sheets.

Bake at 375°F for 10 to 12 minutes or until edges are golden brown and centers are firm to the touch. Remove from cookie sheets; cool on wire racks. Store in tightly covered container for up to 3 days.

Cheese and Spinach Puffs

CHEESE AND SPINACH PUFFS

Yield: 3 to 4 dozen puffs

- *1 (10-ounce) package frozen chopped spinach*
- *½ cup chopped onion*
- *2 eggs*
- *½ cup (2 ounces) shredded Cheddar cheese*
- *⅓ cup Blue cheese salad dressing*
- *2 tablespoons butter, melted*
- *¼ teaspoon garlic powder*
- *1 (8½-ounce) package corn muffin mix*
- *Dijon mustard*

Add onion to frozen spinach; cook as directed on package. Drain well, pressing out liquid.

In medium bowl, beat eggs. Add cheese, salad dressing, butter and garlic powder; mix well. Stir in spinach-onion mixture and muffin mix. Cover; refrigerate 1 hour or until mixture is easy to handle.

Butter cookie sheets. With tablespoon, shape spinach mixture into 1-inch balls; arrange on buttered cookie sheets. Cover; refrigerate or freeze until serving time.

To serve, heat oven to 350°F. Uncover; bake refrigerated puffs for 12 to 15 minutes (frozen puffs for 18 to 20 minutes) or until brown. Serve warm with mustard.

BUTTERY BRAN MUFFINS

Yield: 5 to 6 dozen muffins

- *5 cups all-purpose flour*
- *2 cups sugar*
- *1 cup rolled oats*
- *5 teaspoons baking soda*
- *2 teaspoons salt*
- *1 (15-ounce) box raisin bran cereal*
- *1 quart (4 cups) buttermilk*
- *1 cup (2 sticks) butter, melted*
- *1 cup honey*
- *4 eggs, beaten*

In large bowl, combine all dry ingredients. Add all remaining ingredients; mix well. Cover; store in refrigerator. Batter can be kept in refrigerator for up to 2 weeks.

To bake muffins, heat oven to 400°F. Line muffin cups with paper baking cups. Do not stir batter after being chilled; scoop batter from top. Fill paper-lined muffin cups 2/3 full. Bake at 400°F for 15 to 20 minutes or until golden brown.

◆ ◆ ◆ ◆ ◆ ◆ ◆ ◆ ◆ ◆

Butter cookie sheets and baking pans only when specified in the recipe. To butter a sheet or pan, coat with a thin, even layer of butter using the butter wrapper, plastic wrap, waxed paper or a paper towel for spreading.

◆ ◆ ◆ ◆ ◆ ◆ ◆ ◆ ◆ ◆

Space Needle Restaurant

Seattle, Washington

Where can you savor delicious Northwest cuisine while enjoying one of the world's most spectacular 360-degree views? At the Seattle Space Needle, of course. Ranked as one of the top 20 independent restaurants in the United States, the Space Needle offers a memorable, truly Northwest dining experience.

Enjoy either restaurant on the 500-foot *rotating* level: the Space Needle Restaurant is informal and family-oriented; the Emerald Suite is elegant and intimate. Both offer a variety of dishes including San Juan Prawn Pasta; Emerald City Halibut; and Filet Mignon with glazed wild mushrooms, pearl onions, and Oregon Blue cheese.

In addition, you can delight in mouth-watering appetizers, salads and home-made soups; but always save room for dessert, which includes the Space Needle's famous apple pie.

Before or after your dining experience be sure to visit the recently remodeled Observation Deck at 520 feet which also offers an outer viewing deck. Here you may learn more about the sights of Seattle through Kodak's Compass Northwest display, indulge in a latte from Tully's Coffee, take a photo with Puget Sound and the Olympic Mountains as your backdrop, or take home a souvenir from the gift shop to remember your visit. As always, your elevator ride and Observation Deck visit are complimentary when dining.

Apricot and Pistachio Butter

Yield: 3 cups (1½ pounds)

- 1 *cup peach nectar*
- 1 *cup dried apricots*
- 2 *cups (4 sticks) unsalted butter*
- 2 *tablespoons coarsely chopped shelled pistachios*
- ½ *teaspoon salt*
- ¼ *teaspoon white pepper*

In medium saucepan, combine peach nectar and apricots; cook over medium-high heat for 6 to 8 minutes or until the consistency of light syrup, stirring constantly. Remove from heat; cool.

In food processor bowl with metal blade, process butter until light and fluffy. Add cooled apricot mixture, pistachios, salt and pepper; mix well. Cover; refrigerate until needed.

Use as a flavoring for sauteed vegetables or as an addition to pancakes or French toast.

Space Needle Apple Pie

SPACE NEEDLE APPLE PIE

Yield: 2 (8 or 9-inch) pies; 12 servings

Streusel Topping

- 1 *cup (2 sticks) unsalted butter, softened*
- 1½ *cups all-purpose flour*
- 1½ *cups firmly packed brown sugar*
- 1½ *cups coarsely chopped walnuts*

Filling

- 3 *medium Granny Smith apples, peeled, cored and cut into ¼-inch-thick slices (3 cups)*
- 3 *medium Rome Beauty apples, peeled, cored and cut into ¼-inch-thick slices (3 cups)*
- 2 *tablespoons lemon juice*
- ½ *teaspoon vanilla*
- ½ *cup sugar*
- ¼ *cup all-purpose flour*
- 1 *teaspoon cinnamon*
- ⅛ *teaspoon nutmeg*

Pie Shells

- 2 *(8 or 9-inch) unbaked pie shells*

Heat oven to 350°F. In small bowl with electric mixer, beat butter at low speed for 3 minutes. In medium bowl, combine remaining streusel ingredients; mix well. Add dry ingredients to butter; mix gently until well combined. Set aside.

Place apple slices in large bowl. Sprinkle apples with lemon juice and vanilla; toss well. In medium bowl, combine all remaining filling ingredients; mix well. Add dry ingredients to apple mixture; toss well. Spoon evenly into pie shells; sprinkle each with half of streusel topping.

Bake at 350°F for 40 to 45 minutes or until topping is deep golden brown. Cut each warm pie into six pieces and place on individual plates. Top each slice with warm Apple Cinnamon Caramel Sauce.

APPLE CINNAMON CARAMEL SAUCE

Yield: 3 cups

- 4 *cups apple juice*
- 1 *ounce (¼ cup) dried apples, minced*
- 1½ *cups (3 sticks) unsalted butter*
- ½ *teaspoon cinnamon*

In medium saucepan, combine apple juice and apples; cook over high heat for about 20 minutes or until the consistency of light syrup, stirring occasionally.

Remove saucepan from heat; slowly beat in small amounts of butter until all has been incorporated. Beat in cinnamon. (This mixture is sensitive to heat. Avoid excessive cold or hot temperatures.)

To serve, drizzle 1/4 cup sauce over wedge of warm Space Needle Apple Pie.

♦ ♦ ♦ ♦ ♦ ♦ ♦ ♦ ♦ ♦

Many chefs prefer unsalted butter for seafood and baking because of its delicate flavor.

★

Stir a pat of butter into a sauce during the last minute of cooking for a rich buttery taste and glossy appearance.

♦ ♦ ♦ ♦ ♦ ♦ ♦ ♦ ♦ ♦

MIDWEST

Stretching from Ohio to Iowa, and continuing from North Dakota to Oklahoma, the Midwest is the geographic center of the country. This massive area is the home of the mighty Mississippi River and the Great Lakes, as well as farmhouses and silos dotting endless stretches of corn and grain fields. Here, too, is the heart of country's homestyle cooking — warm pot pies, fresh breads and biscuits, and hearty meat and potatoes dishes. It's the kind of cooking that has made family picnics and church suppers American institutions.

Hundreds of years ago, the Great Lakes and numerous other waterways provided natives with ample supplies of trout, perch, bass, smelt and wild rice. Even to this day, the Chippewa people harvest wild rice in the same way their ancestors did — in canoes using cedar sticks. In the 1600's, French explorers traveled south from Canada searching for the Northwest Passage to the Orient. Instead, they encountered excellent farmland and Native Americans eager to engage in fur trading.

But it was a relentless immigration of different cultures from the Eastern United States as well as Europe that shaped the cuisine and economy of the Midwest. The fertile soils of Illinois, Indiana, Ohio and southern Michigan were eagerly cultivated by these new arrivals who planted corn, wheat, rye and garden vegetables such as squash, beans and cabbage. Amish and Mennonite groups also began to migrate westward from Pennsylvania in the 1830's, and they brought cows and pigs with them. The Ukrainian Mennonites moved even farther west, and planted the drought-resistant corn that transformed Kansas into America's breadbasket. Germans worked alongside the Danes and Norwegians in Missouri and Iowa. In addition to developing grain crops, the Germans established a long tradition of animal husbandry in Iowa and the Plains states, and when the railroad arrived in 1867, Iowa and her neighbors could finally send their bounty well beyond their borders.

In addition to beef, grain and corn, the Midwest is also a fertile ground for dairy products. In fact, Wisconsin bills itself as "America's Dairyland," where one and a half million cows reside. And the cows are very busy. In 1994, they produced over 22 billion pounds of milk. The state leads the country in cheese production and accounts for one-quarter of the country's Butter output.

GRAY GOOSE INN

Chesterton, Indiana

The Gray Goose Inn is located in the charming town of Chesterton, Indiana. The Inn was originally built on a 300 acre parcel of land as the home of the Schneider family. The property, which included a beautiful lake, was named "Palomara Farm" and the lake "Palomara Lake." The name Palomara was created by combining the first two letters of his children's names. Pat, Lon, Mary and Ray. The family enjoyed this truly idyllic property. Summers were spent boating, fishing and horseback riding. On autumn nights the family enjoyed moonlit hay rides. The winter months were filled with sleigh rides, midnight ice skating and bonfires.

As the years passed and the children married and moved on, Mr. Schneider decided to sell the property. In July of 1986 the house and three acres became known as the Gray Goose Inn. Decorated in traditional English decor with lots of fresh flowers the Inn became known for its sincere and friendly hospitality. Each of the Inns rooms are beautifully decorated and designed for the utmost in comfort.

Breakfast time is a special time at the Gray Goose. As the first rays of sun glisten over Lake Palomara, you awaken to the aromas of their gourmet breakfast prepared especially for you. It is served graciously in their Dining Room with its walls and shelves covered with unusual plates and mugs. A cozy fire burns in the library, next to the dining room several months during the year.

The grounds provide wooded scenic walking trails, paddle boats and bird watching. Both rooms have large windows facing the lake.

The Inn is close to Dunes State Park and National Lakeshore where guests can swim, enjoy nature walks, hiking and picnicking. The Gray Goose Inn has been recognized for its excellence by many magazines, local newspapers and The American Bed and Breakfast Association.

Whatever your reason for staying at the Inn, be it pleasure or business, the moment you enter through its doors you will sense the qualities that set the Gray Goose apart from the ordinary.

EASY AND QUICK CORN BREAD PUDDING

Yield: 12 servings

- 2 *(15-ounce) cans whole kernel corn, drained*
- 2 *(15-ounce) cans cream style corn*
- 2 *(8½-ounce) packages corn bread mix*
- 1 *cup (2 sticks) butter, melted*

Heat oven to 350°F. Butter 13x9-inch pan. In large bowl, combine all ingredients; mix until well blended. Pour into buttered pan. Bake at 350°F for 1 hour or until edges are golden brown and toothpick inserted in center comes out clean.

Easy Buttery Pound Cake

EASY BUTTERY POUND CAKE

Yield: 10 to 12 servings

- 1 *cup (2 sticks) butter, softened*
- 1 *(8-ounce) package cream cheese, softened*
- 1½ *cups sugar*
- 4 *eggs*
- 1½ *teaspoons vanilla*
- 1¾ *cups all-purpose flour*
- 1½ *teaspoons baking powder*

Heat oven to 350°F. Butter and flour 12-cup Bundt pan. In large bowl, combine butter and cream cheese; beat until creamy. Add sugar; beat 5 minutes. Add eggs one at a time, beating well after each addition. Stir in vanilla. Add flour and baking powder; mix well. Pour into buttered and floured pan.

Bake at 350°F for 50 to 60 minutes or until golden brown and toothpick inserted in center comes out clean. Cool upright in pan 25 minutes. Remove from pan. Cool completely.

SOUTH OF THE BORDER EGG BAKE

Yield: 12 servings

- 12 *eggs*
- ½ *cup all-purpose flour*
- 1 *teaspoon baking powder*
- ½ *teaspoon salt, if desired*
- 1 *pound (4 cups) Monterey Jack cheese, shredded*
- 1½ *pints (3 cups) small curd cottage cheese*
- ½ *cup (1 stick) butter, softened*
- 4 *ounces fresh (hot or mild) green chiles, seeded, chopped, or*
- 1 *(4½-ounce) can chopped green chiles, drained*
- 1 *(2-ounce) jar chopped pimiento, drained*
- 1 *(7-ounce) can whole kernel corn, drained*

Heat oven to 350°F. Butter 13x9-inch (3-quart) baking dish. In large bowl, beat eggs until light. Add all remaining ingredients; mix well. Pour into buttered dish.

Bake in 350°F for 45 to 55 minutes or until puffy, brown and knife inserted in center comes out clean. Serve hot.

◆ ◆ ◆ ◆ ◆ ◆ ◆ ◆ ◆ ◆

To evenly distribute spices and flavorings in a batter, cream them with butter.

★

Baked goods made with butter generally stay fresh and moist longer.

◆ ◆ ◆ ◆ ◆ ◆ ◆ ◆ ◆ ◆

THE GOLDEN LAMB INN

Lebanon, Ohio

The Golden Lamb Inn is located in the historic town of Lebanon, Ohio. The Inn is Ohio's oldest and has been host to Charles Dickens, Mark Twain, Henry Clay, Harriet Stowe, and ten United States Presidents.

The eighteen guest rooms are charmingly decorated with antiques and are named after a particular famous visitor from the past.

The Inn serves typical American cuisine in its public dining room and offers five smaller dining rooms for private parties.

The town of Lebanon boasts many classic Greek revival homes and buildings and guests are encouraged to visit all the town's historic sites. Of particular note is the Warren County Historical Society Museum located two doors south of the Inn. Interested patrons will find a completely restored 19th century village, complete with displays, shops and costumed mannequins. The area has numerous antique shops for those guests wishing to own a piece of history. The area also offers many outdoor activities such as hiking, canoeing, and biking.

As a guest of the Golden Lamb Inn you will be graciously treated with hospitality drenched in almost two hundred years of tradition.

OLD-FASHIONED POTATO SOUP

Yield: 10 (1 ½-cup) servings

- ¼ *cup (½ stick) butter*
- 2 *leeks, sliced (1 cup)*
- 1 *onion, chopped (1 cup)*
- 1 *tablespoon all-purpose flour*
- 1 *quart (4 cups) chicken broth*
- 2 *pounds potatoes, peeled, diced (7 cups)*
- 2 *cups milk*
- 2 *cups half-and-half*
- ½ *teaspoon salt*
- ¼ *teaspoon pepper*
- ⅛ *teaspoon dried marjoram leaves*
- ⅛ *teaspoon dried thyme leaves*

Melt butter in Dutch oven or large sauce pot over medium-high heat. Add leeks and onion; cook until transparent. Stir in flour until well mixed. Add broth. Bring to a boil, stirring constantly until slightly thickened. Add potatoes. Reduce heat to low; simmer 20 to 25 minutes or until potatoes are tender. Add all remaining ingredients; cook until thoroughly heated.

Praline Crème Pie

PRALINE CRÈME PIE

Yield: 8 servings

<u>*Praline*</u>

- ½ *cup (1 stick) butter*
- ⅓ *cup firmly packed brown sugar*
- ½ *cup pecans*

<u>*Pie Shell*</u>

- 1 *(9-inch) baked pie shell*

<u>*Butterscotch Crème*</u>

- ⅔ *cup firmly packed brown sugar*
- 2 *tablespoons cornstarch*
- ⅛ *teaspoon salt*
- 2 *cups milk*
- 2 *egg yolks*
- 2 *tablespoons butter, softened*
- 2 *teaspoons vanilla*

For praline mixture, in small saucepan, combine all praline ingredients. Bring to a boil over medium-high heat, stirring constantly. Pour into baked pie shell. Cool until set.

To prepare butterscotch crème, in medium saucepan, combine brown sugar, cornstarch and salt. In small bowl, combine milk and egg yolks; beat well. Gradually stir into sugar mixture. Cook over medium heat, stirring constantly, just until thickened and bubbly. Stir in butter and vanilla. Pour over praline mixture in pie shell. Refrigerate at least 4 hours before serving. Top with whipped cream before serving.

GOLDEN LAMB'S CHICKEN POT PIE

Yield: 6 servings

- 2 *prepared unbaked pie crusts*
- 1 *quart (4 cups) chicken broth*
- ½ *teaspoon salt*
- ¼ *teaspoon pepper*
- 8 *tablespoons (1 stick) butter*
- ½ *cup all-purpose flour*
- ½ *cup half-and-half*
- ¾ *teaspoon crushed dried rosemary leaves*
- 1½ *cups sliced fresh mushrooms*
- 1 *cup diced celery*
- ¾ *pound (2 cups) diced cooked chicken*
- 2½ *cups diced cooked potatoes*

Heat oven to 450°F. Butter 6 individual casseroles. Cut pie crusts to fit tops of casseroles. Place on unbuttered cookie sheet; prick generously with fork. Bake at 450°F for 9 minutes or until light brown.

Meanwhile, in large saucepan, bring chicken broth to a boil; add salt and pepper. Set aside; keep warm. In another large saucepan, melt 4 tablespoons of the butter over medium heat. Stir in flour, cooking and stirring for about 5 minutes; do not brown. Add seasoned chicken broth, half-and-half and rosemary, stirring constantly until thickened. Set aside; keep warm.

In medium skillet, melt remaining 4 tablespoons butter over medium-high heat. Add mushrooms and celery; cook until tender without browning. Stir in chicken and potatoes. Spoon evenly into buttered casseroles. Ladle scant 1 cup sauce over chicken and vegetables. Place partially baked crust over each casserole.

Reduce oven temperature to 375°F. Bake 15 to 20 minutes or until mixture is bubbly and crust is golden brown.

◆ ◆ ◆ ◆ ◆ ◆ ◆ ◆ ◆ ◆

Fresh mushrooms will keep for up to 5 days if stored in a moisture-proof container.

★

Do not wash mushrooms until ready for use. Dry thoroughly.

★

To ensure the right consistency of whipped cream, chill the beaters and bowl in the freezer before beating. The cream should be well chilled, too.

◆ ◆ ◆ ◆ ◆ ◆ ◆ ◆ ◆ ◆

EAGLE RIDGE INN & RESORT

Galena, Illinois

Eagle Ridge Inn & Resort is located on 6,800 rolling, wooded acres in the scenic northwestern Illinois town of Galena. Built in 1978, Eagle Ridge Inn is known as "The Inn Resort for Golf."

The Inn is located in the center of the resort and provides eighty charming guest rooms and suites, each one individually decorated and featuring lake or woodland views, fireplaces, four-poster beds, jacuzzis and balconies. Lodging options also include 350 one-to-five bedroom Resort Villas hidden away in the rolling hills of Eagle Ridge for your privacy and serenity. Each villa is fully furnished and equipped with every convenience.

This year-round family resort features 63 holes of championship golf, tennis, horseback riding, biking, hiking, boating, fishing, children's programs, cross-country skiing, skating and sledding.

Indoor fun includes a complete fitness facility with pool, whirlpool, sauna and exercise equipment.

Dining options range from the country elegance of Woodlands Restaurant overlooking beautiful Lake Galena, to casual dining at the Clubhouse Bar and Grill, to the old-fashioned fun of Scoops Ice Cream Parlor.

Visiting historic Galena just a short drive from Eagle Ridge is like stepping back in time. This 19th century lead-mining boom-town has preserved its colorful past in its architecture and museums.

Galena was also home to Ulysses S. Grant, and his post-Civil War home, furnished with Grant family heirlooms, is open to the public.

Visitors may also enjoy many galleries, over 230 antique shops and specialty stores, tours of historic homes and cruises along the mighty Mississippi on authentic paddle wheelers.

After visiting Eagle Ridge Inn & Resort, you will understand why it is known as one of the top family resorts in America.

CORN AND SAUSAGE CHOWDER

Yield: 10 (1-cup) servings

- 3 *tablespoons butter*
- ⅔ *cup chopped onions*
- ¼ *cup diced celery*
- 6 *tablespoons all-purpose flour*
- 5 *cups chicken broth*
- 1 *cup diced potatoes*
- 1 *(1-pound) package frozen corn*
- 5½ *ounces (1¼ cups) sliced or diced lean spicy or Southwestern sausage*
- 1½ *cups heavy cream*
- ¼ *teaspoon salt*
- ⅛ *teaspoon pepper*

In large saucepan, melt butter. Add onions and celery; cook until tender, but not brown. Add flour; cook and stir slowly for 4 to 5 minutes. Do not brown mixture. Add broth; mix well. Add potatoes; simmer about 20 minutes or until vegetables are tender.

Add corn and sausage; simmer an additional 20 minutes. Stir in heavy cream, salt and pepper.

Cheddar Cheese Scones

CHEDDAR CHEESE SCONES

Yield: 16 servings

- 5 *cups all-purpose flour*
- 3 *tablespoons sugar*
- 6 *teaspoons baking powder*
- ½ *teaspoon salt*
- ¾ *cup (1½ sticks) butter*
- 1½ *cups heavy cream*
- 4 *eggs, beaten*
- ¼ *cup (1 ounce) shredded Cheddar cheese*
- 3 *tablespoons finely chopped green onions*
- 1 *tablespoon grated Parmesan cheese*

Butter 1 large or 2 small cookie sheets. In large bowl, combine flour, sugar, baking powder and salt; mix well. With pastry blender or fork, cut in butter until mixture resembles coarse crumbs. Add cream, eggs, Cheddar cheese and onions; blend until all ingredients are combined. Let dough rest at least 35 minutes.

Heat oven to 375°F. If desired, divide dough into 2 parts. Knead dough about 10 times; roll out to a round about 3/4 inch thick. Place on buttered cookie sheet; sprinkle top with Parmesan cheese. Score large round into 16 wedges or small rounds into 8 wedges each.

Bake at 375°F for 35 to 38 minutes or until deep golden brown. Cut into wedges; serve immediately.

CHOCOLATE NUT COOKIES

Yield: 6 dozen (3-inch) cookies

- 1½ *cups (3 sticks) butter*
- 1½ *cups sugar*
- 1 *cup firmly packed light brown sugar*
- 4 *eggs*
- 4 *teaspoons vanilla*
- 4⅔ *cups all-purpose flour*
- 2½ *teaspoons baking powder*
- 1 *pound (4 cups) chopped pecans or walnuts*
- 1 *pound 12 ounces chopped Swiss chocolate*

In large bowl, combine butter, sugar and brown sugar; beat until well blended. Add eggs and vanilla; beat well. Add flour and baking powder; mix well. Stir in pecans and chocolate. Shape dough into rolls, 2 to 2 1/2 inches in diameter. Wrap rolls in plastic wrap; refrigerate until firm.

When ready to bake, heat oven to 350°F. Butter cookie sheets. Cut rolls into 1/4-inch-thick slices; place on buttered cookie sheets. Bake at 350°F for 8 to 9 minutes or until cookies are just set and bottoms are light, golden brown.

♦ ♦ ♦ ♦ ♦ ♦ ♦ ♦ ♦ ♦

To soften butter in a microwave oven, microwave 1 stick on the lowest power setting, checking every 30 seconds. If the butter is inadvertently melted, use it for another purpose. Melted butter is unsuitable for cookies and most other baked goods.

♦ ♦ ♦ ♦ ♦ ♦ ♦ ♦ ♦ ♦

Southwest

The beauty and grandeur of the Southwest are complemented by an equally unique cuisine. The mountains, flat top mesas, and vast deserts, endless blue skies and other natural wonders are unlike those in any other part of the country. And the Southwest's distinctive cuisine perfectly reflects the varied landscape. The food is boldly flavored. And its colors — bright red, yellow and green chilies, slate blue corn — mirror the hues that paint the horizon.

Spanish and Native Americans lived together in the region for nearly 200 years without other outside interference. This interaction formed the basis for modern Southwest cooking. During this period, unique varieties of native corn and beans were incorporated into Spanish dishes, as were cacti, pine nuts and squashes. The Spanish considerably broadened the diet, though, bringing such new items as peaches, apricots and apples. They grew wheat to make flour for breads and tortillas. And Spanish missionaries led herds of cattle and sheep up from Mexico, adding beef, milk and cheese to the local diet.

But most importantly, Spanish colonists began to cultivate chile peppers on a large scale, and their fiery flavors became a trademark of Southwest cooking. And these same colonists also influenced not only what was eaten, but how food was consumed. They introduced the custom of serving appetizers, such as nachos and quesadillas, and made the Southwest a paradise for lovers of small dishes.

The settling of Texas in the mid-1800's also had a profound effect on the cuisine of the region. After the Civil War, the new western lifestyle on the Texas ranges meant cattle drives. Millions of animals, descendants of the original Spanish herds, moved across the state. And during these "chuckwagon" journeys, hearty meals were prepared for the cowboys to sustain them through long days in the saddle. The cowboy influence remains vital today to the identity of Texas cuisine. The chuckwagon custom of cooking and grilling over an open fire has inspired a thriving barbecue tradition — the region's most enduring cooking technique.

It is no surprise then, that food of the American Southwest has been embraced by people and chefs from across the country. Certainly, the heat of superhot chilies is a large part of the appeal. But more importantly, there is something enchanting in these rough, pure flavors. When it's all said and done, the elements of Southwest cooking are not complicated, but once combined, are enchanting.

Dos Casas Viejas

Santa Fe, New Mexico

Dos Casas Viejas is located in the heart of the historic Guadalupe district of Old Santa Fe, New Mexico. The Bed and Breakfast opened in 1990 and consists of a collection of intimate and charming adobe buildings. Housed within a walled and gated half-acre, the compound provides each guest with the opportunity to experience the character, charm and tradition found in Santa Fe during the 1860's. The main building includes the beautifully decorated lobby/library and lovely patio.

Each casita is designed to provide the utmost in comfort and privacy. All have private entry gates, and secluded, landscaped patios. Each of the private adobe walled patios is furnished with custom-built willow furniture with luxurious cushions providing the ultimate spot for relaxing.

Lovely french doors open into beautifully decorated casitas. Each casita includes a kiva fireplace, cable TV, private telephones and answering machines; and fresh flowers.

All rooms are unique in that they provide a "1860's" Santa Fe ambiance and are exquisitely decorated with period furnishings and yet, provide the guest with state of the art amenities.

The Inn has a wonderful 40-foot pool with a large patio for alfresco dining or lounging.

Dos Casa Viejas serves a delicious continental breakfast "plus" in their graciously decorated dining room.

All of Sante Fe is historic and offers visitors history and fine art museums in its downtown "Old Plaza" district. Visitors may also enjoy Canyon Road, and old historic buildings converted into over 150 galleries and shops. Santa Fe National Forest comprises an area of one and a half million acres of wilderness perfect for hiking, camping and skiing.

Dos Casa Viejas, along with the historic atmosphere of Santa Fe, provides guests with a true sense of the "Old Southwest" combined with all the comfort, sophistication and culture of the "New Southwest."

Oatmeal Scones

Yield: 8 servings

Scones

- 1¾ *cups all-purpose flour*
- ⅓ *cup sugar*
- 1½ *teaspoons baking powder*
- ¾ *teaspoons baking soda*
- ½ *teaspoon salt*
- 1 *teaspoon grated orange peel (1 large orange)*
- ½ *cup (1 stick) unsalted butter, chilled, cut into pieces*
- 1⅓ *cups quick-cooking rolled oats*
- ½ *cup raisins*
- 1 *cup buttermilk*

Topping

- 1 *egg, beaten*
- 1 *tablespoon sugar*

Heat oven to 375°F. In food processor bowl with metal blade, combine flour, sugar, baking powder, baking soda, salt and grated orange peel; process until well blended. Add butter; process until mixture resembles coarse meal. Transfer to large bowl; stir in oats, raisins and buttermilk just until sticky dough forms. Lightly butter large cookie sheet.

On lightly floured surface with floured hands, knead dough 10 times. Gather dough into 8 handfuls and place on buttered cookie sheet; flatten each slightly. Brush with beaten egg; sprinkle with sugar.

Bake at 375°F for 20 to 25 minutes or until golden brown.

Blueberry Coffee Cake

BLUEBERRY COFFEE CAKE

Yield: 9 servings

Cake
- ½ cup (1 stick) butter, softened
- ¾ cup sugar
- ½ cup milk
- 1 egg
- 2 cups all-purpose flour
- 2 teaspoons baking powder
- ½ teaspoon salt
- 1½ to 2½ cups blueberries

Topping
- ⅔ cup firmly packed brown sugar
- ½ cup all-purpose flour
- 1 teaspoon cinnamon
- 6 tablespoons butter
- ½ cup chopped walnuts

Heat oven to 375°F. Butter 9-inch square pan. To prepare cake, in large mixer bowl, beat butter and sugar until well blended. Add milk and egg. In small bowl, combine flour, baking powder and salt. Add to butter mixture; stir just until combined. Fold in blueberries. Pour batter into buttered pan.

To prepare topping, combine all topping ingredients in food processor bowl with metal blade; process until combined. Sprinkle evenly over batter.

Bake at 375°F for 45 to 50 minutes or until toothpick inserted in center comes out clean. Cool 20 to 30 minutes before serving.

COFFEE PECAN MUFFINS

Yield: 1 dozen muffins

- 1 cup pecans
- 1¾ cups all-purpose flour
- ½ cup firmly packed dark brown sugar
- 3 teaspoons baking powder
- ¼ teaspoon salt
- 1 egg
- ½ cup milk
- ½ cup (1 stick) butter, melted
- 2 tablespoons strong coffee
- 1 teaspoon vanilla

Heat oven to 400°F. Butter 12 muffin cups.

Reserve 12 pecan halves for muffin tops. Coarsely chop remaining pecans; set aside. In large bowl, combine flour, brown sugar, baking powder and salt; mix well. In another bowl, lightly beat egg. Add milk, butter, coffee and vanilla; blend well. Add liquid mixture to flour mixture; mix just until combined. Fold in chopped pecans. Spoon batter into buttered muffin cups; top with reserved pecan halves.

Bake at 400°F for 16 to 20 minutes or until toothpick inserted in center comes out clean. Serve warm.

◆ ◆ ◆ ◆ ◆ ◆ ◆ ◆ ◆ ◆

To soften brown sugar, cover tightly with plastic wrap and microwave on HIGH for 20 seconds. Do not overheat.

★

Before beginning, read a recipe thoroughly and assemble the ingredients.

◆ ◆ ◆ ◆ ◆ ◆ ◆ ◆ ◆ ◆

THE LODGE AT SEDONA

Sedona, Arizona

The Lodge at Sedona is located in the breathtaking town of Sedona, Arizona. The town of Sedona was named after Sedona Schnebly, who, in 1902 with her husband Carl, followed their dreams by leaving their home in Missouri and moving to a settlement in Arizona called Upper Creek. Once settled in their new state they operated a hotel, where Sedona became renowned for her cooking and hospitality. Subsequently, this small community was named Sedona.

Ninety years later Mark and Barb Dinunzio followed their dreams by moving to Sedona and opened a Bed and Breakfast of their own, calling it The Lodge at Sedona.

In their own words, Mark and Barb said: "We operate as a classic Bed and Breakfast, but the generous size of our Inn allows people to spread out and enjoy the peace and quiet..."

The Inn has thirteen beautifully appointed guest rooms and suites, several with private outdoor decks, brick fireplaces, and mountain or wooded views. The Inn's rustic sitting rooms, fireside parlors, and library are all accented with rough-hewn timbers and native sandstone.

A sumptuous breakfast and afternoon appetizers, complemented by the majestic views of Sedona's spectacular red rocks, is only part of what makes The Lodge at Sedona so special.

Guests may enjoy many of the fascinating points of interest that surround the Sedona area. The dramatic surroundings of canyons and rock formations of red sandstone and white limestone provide spectacular jeep tours, hiking, and mountain biking. Ancient Indian ruins and a ghost mining town allow visitors a fascinating glimpse into the history of the west. Sedona is renowned for its numerous art galleries and the Jazz on the Rocks festival in September. The Grand Canyon is a two hour drive away.

The Lodge at Sedona reflects all the love and creativity that Mark and Barb have poured into it. Over the years the Inn has been the recipient of many awards for its outstanding accommodations and hospitality.

CORN, JALAPEÑO AND PEANUT SOUP

Yield: 4 (1 ¼-cup) servings

- 5 *tablespoons butter*
- ¾ *cup diced celery*
- ½ *cup diced onion*
- ½ *cup diced red bell pepper*
- 2 *teaspoons diced jalapeño chile*
- ½ *cup chunky-style peanut butter*
- 1 *(14 ½-ounce) can chicken broth*
- 1½ *cups frozen whole kernel corn*
- 1 *cup heavy cream*
- ¼ *cup chopped fresh cilantro*

In large saucepan, melt 3 tablespoons of the butter over medium-high heat. Add celery, onion, bell pepper and jalapeño chile; cook until tender and onion is slightly browned. Stir in peanut butter; cook, stirring constantly, until melted. Add chicken broth and corn. Reduce heat; simmer 15 minutes.

Remove saucepan from heat; stir in cream. Quickly stir in remaining 2 tablespoons butter until melted. Ladle soup into 4 individual soup bowls; sprinkle with cilantro.

Spoon Bread

SPOON BREAD

Yield: 8 to 10 servings

- 2 *shallots, finely chopped*
- 2 *garlic cloves, minced*
- 1½ *tablespoons chopped canned green chiles*
- 2 *cups milk*
- 1 *cup cornmeal*
- 1 *cup (4 ounces) shredded Monterey Jack cheese*
- 1 *cup (4 ounces) shredded Cheddar cheese*
- 1 *cup (2 sticks) unsalted butter*
- ¼ *cup maple syrup*
- *Salt to taste*
- 5 *eggs, separated*

In medium saucepan, combine shallots, garlic, chiles and milk; bring just to a boil over medium-high heat. Gradually add cornmeal, stirring constantly. Reduce heat; cook about 5 minutes or until thickened, stirring occasionally.

Remove saucepan from heat; stir in cheeses, butter, syrup and salt until well combined. Set aside to cool.

Heat oven to 350°F. Butter 2-quart casserole. In small bowl, beat egg yolks; stir into cooled cornmeal mixture. In another small bowl, beat egg whites until stiff peaks form; fold into mixture. Pour into buttered casserole. Cover.

Bake at 350°F for 50 to 60 minutes or until deep golden brown and knife inserted in center comes out clean. Serve immediately.

BANANA FOSTER CHEESECAKE SQUARES

Yield: 24 servings

<u>Crust</u>

- 1½ *cups graham cracker crumbs*
- 6 *tablespoons sugar*
- ½ *cup (1 stick) butter, melted*

<u>Cheesecake</u>

- 3 *pounds cream cheese, softened*
- 1½ *cups firmly packed brown sugar*
- 3 *tablespoons cornstarch*
- 1½ *teaspoons cinnamon*
- 6 *eggs*
- 2 *egg yolks*
- 1⅓ *cups pureed bananas*
- 6 *tablespoons rum*
- 4 *teaspoons vanilla*

Heat oven to 325°F. In small bowl, combine graham cracker crumbs, sugar and butter until well mixed. Press evenly in bottom of 15x10x1-inch baking pan.

In large bowl, combine cream cheese, brown sugar, cornstarch and cinnamon until smooth. Add eggs and egg yolks one at a time, beating well after each addition. Beat in all remaining ingredients. Pour into crust-lined pan. (Pan will be very full.)

Bake at 325°F for 55 to 65 minutes or until center is firm to the touch. Cool completely before serving. Store in refrigerator.

♦ ♦ ♦ ♦ ♦ ♦ ♦ ♦ ♦ ♦

Store garlic in a cool, dry place. If refrigerated, keep in a tightly closed glass container to prevent odor from permeating other foods.

To peel cloves of garlic easily, firmly press the cloves with the handle of a knife to break the skin.

♦ ♦ ♦ ♦ ♦ ♦ ♦ ♦ ♦ ♦

THE INN ABOVE ONION CREEK

Kyle, Texas

◆ ◆ ◆ ◆ ◆ ◆ ◆ ◆ ◆ ◆ ◆ ◆ ◆ ◆ ◆ ◆ ◆

The Inn Above Onion Creek is located between Kyle and the rural southwestern town of Wimberley, Texas. Wimberley is located on Cyprus Creek and has been described as a true pioneer town.

The Inn is situated on 500 acres in the spectacular Texas Hills. Built to look old and rustic, the Inn opened its doors for guests in 1994. Although the setting is appropriately rural and rustic, the accommodations are luxurious and gracious. As a guest you have a choice of six delightful guest rooms, each with its own spacious bath. All rooms are beautifully furnished and offer the utmost in comfort. Each guest room has its own fireplace for added coziness. The Inn also has a well-stocked library for your reading pleasure. There is also a new swimming pool and miles of trails for hiking.

Full breakfasts are served hearthside and include fresh fruit, homemade breads and pastries, pancakes and french toast. In the evenings, as you watch a multi-hued hill country sunset from the Inn's westward porch, the Inn serves a light supper of fresh-baked breads, homemade soups and fresh salads.

The area surrounding The Inn Above Onion Creek is breathtaking. The San Marcos River and Canyon Lake offer fishing, tubing and rafting. The many beautiful hills such as "Old Baldie" are a favorite for climbing for their spectacular views. Austin and San Antonio are within an hour's drive as well as the National Wildflower Research Center and Johnson City's "Lyndon Johnson National Historic Park."

German settlers had a tremendous influence in Texas and the nearby town of New Braunfels offers the charmingly restored German Victorian community of Gruene. Another tourist favorite is Market Day, held the first Saturday in April through December, in Wimberley. Visitors can shop for wonderful antiques and crafts.

A visit at The Inn Above Onion Creek offers its guests the atmosphere of the Old West, the invigorating pleasures of the great outdoors with all the luxuries and accommodations one would expect from a hill country retreat.

◆ ◆

OVEN FRENCH TOAST

Yield: 8 servings

- 1 *cup firmly packed brown sugar*
- ½ *cup (1 stick) butter*
- 1 *tablespoon light corn syrup*
- 1 *loaf French bread, diagonally cut into 16 (1-inch-thick) slices*
- 5 *eggs*
- 2 *cups milk*
- 1 *teaspoon cinnamon*
- 1 *teaspoon nutmeg*
- 1 *teaspoon vanilla*
- ¼ *cup chopped pecans, if desired*

In medium bowl with pastry blender, combine brown sugar, butter and corn syrup until well mixed. Press in bottom of unbuttered 15x10x1-inch baking pan. Place bread slices over brown sugar mixture.

In another medium bowl, beat eggs, milk, cinnamon, nutmeg and vanilla until well blended. Pour evenly over bread. Cover; refrigerate overnight.

Heat oven to 350°F. Sprinkle with pecans. Bake 30 to 35 minutes or until light golden brown. If desired, serve with fruit or yogurt and bacon.

Rich Blueberry Pancakes

RICH BLUEBERRY PANCAKES

Yield: 9 (5¾-inch) pancakes

- 1½ *cups all-purpose flour*
- 6 *tablespoons sugar*
- 2½ *teaspoons baking powder*
- 2 *teaspoons baking soda*
- 3 *eggs*
- 1½ *cups buttermilk*
- 1½ *teaspoons vanilla*
- ½ *cup (1 stick) butter, melted*
- ¾ *cup blueberries*

In small bowl, combine flour, sugar, baking powder and baking soda; mix well. In large bowl with electric mixer, combine eggs, buttermilk, vanilla and melted butter; beat until well blended. Add dry ingredients; beat until smooth. Stir in blueberries.

Heat griddle to 375°F or skillet over medium heat until drop of water bubbles and bounces on surface. For each pancake, pour 1/2 cup batter onto hot griddle. Cook 5 to 7 minutes or until bubbles appear on surface of pancakes and bottoms are light golden brown. Turn pancakes; cook 3 to 5 minutes or until light golden brown. Serve immediately. (If desired, recipe can be doubled.)

OATMEAL CAKE

Yield: 15 servings

Cake

- 1¼ *cups boiling water*
- 1 *cup quick oats*
- ½ *cup (1 stick) butter, softened*
- 2 *eggs*
- 2 *cups sugar*
- 1 *cup firmly packed brown sugar*
- 1½ *cups all-purpose flour*
- 1 *teaspoon baking soda*
- ½ to 1 *teaspoon cinnamon*

Topping

- ½ *cup sugar*
- 1 *cup coconut*
- 1 *cup evaporated milk*
- 1 *cup pecans, chopped*

In large bowl, pour boiling water over oats and butter. Let stand 30 minutes, stirring occasionally.

Heat oven to 350°F. Butter 13x9x2-inch pan. In small bowl, beat eggs; add to oat mixture. Add sugar and brown sugar; mix well. Sift together flour, baking soda and cinnamon; stir into oat mixture. Pour batter into buttered pan.

Bake at 350°F for 30 minutes.

In medium bowl, combine all topping ingredients; pour over hot cake in pan. Return to oven; brown an additional 15 to 20 minutes.

◆ ◆ ◆ ◆ ◆ ◆ ◆ ◆ ◆ ◆

If butter cakes are refrigerated or frozen, bring to room temperature before serving for the best texture and flavor (cakes made with whipped cream and other perishable fillings and frostings should be thawed in the refrigerator and served cold).

Test baking soda for freshness: Add 1/4 teaspoon baking soda to 1 tablespoon vinegar or lemon juice. If it bubbles, the baking soda is fresh.

◆ ◆ ◆ ◆ ◆ ◆ ◆ ◆ ◆ ◆

★ ★ ★ ★ ★ ★ ★ ★ ★ ★ ★

The Woodstock Inn & Resort

10% Discount
Off Room Rate

With Minimum 2 Night Stay
Mention The Seasonal Celebrations Across America Cookbook When Making Your Reservation!

Fourteen The Green
Woodstock, Vermont 05091-1298
Telephone (800) 448-7900
Offer Expires 12/31/97

★ ★ ★ ★ ★ ★ ★ ★ ★ ★ ★

★ ★ ★ ★ ★ ★ ★ ★ ★ ★ ★

The Queen Victoria®

Special Rate
For Any Two Night Stay
(Monday - Thursday),
November 1996 - March 1997

Dane & Joan Wells, Innkeepers
102 Ocean Street, Cape May, NJ 08204
Telephone 609-884-8702

★ ★ ★ ★ ★ ★ ★ ★ ★ ★ ★

★ ★ ★ ★ ★ ★ ★ ★ ★ ★ ★

Gray Goose Inn

350 Indian Boundary Road
Chesterton, Indiana 46304
Telephone (219) 926-5781

Upgrade
From Any Room to
Suite
(Excluding Weekends & Holidays)
Offer Expires 12/31/97

★ ★ ★ ★ ★ ★ ★ ★ ★ ★ ★

★ ★ ★ ★ ★ ★ ★ ★ ★ ★ ★

10% Off
Food Bill
At The Grain House
Restaurant

225 Route 202
Basking Ridge, NJ 07920
Telephone 908-221-1100
Offer Expires 12/31/97

★ ★ ★ ★ ★ ★ ★ ★ ★ ★ ★

★ ★ ★ ★ ★ ★ ★ ★ ★ ★ ★

125 Kallof Place
Sedona, Arizona 86336
Telephone (800) 619-4467
www.sedona.net/bb/lodge

10% Discount
Off Room Rate

With Minimum 2 Night Stay
Offer Expires 12/31/97

★ ★ ★ ★ ★ ★ ★ ★ ★ ★ ★

Deerfield Inn
The Street
Deerfield, Massachusetts 01342
Telephone (413) 774-5587

★

Griswold Inn
36 Main Street
Essex, Connecticut 06426
Telephone (860) 767-1776

★

Hartness House Inn
30 Orchard Street
Springfield, Vermont 05156
Telephone (802) 885-2115

★

Beekman 1766 Tavern
4 Mill Street
Rhinebeck, New York 12572
Telephone (914) 871-1766

★

Asa Ransom House
10529 Main Street
Clarence, New York 14031
Telephone (716) 759-2315

Clifton - The Country Inn
1296 Clifton Inn Drive
Charlottesville, Virginia 22911
Telephone (804) 971-1800

★

Opryland Hotel
2800 Opryland Drive
Nashville, Tennessee 37214
Telephone (615) 871-7859

★

Camberley's Martha Washington Inn
150 West Main Street
Abingdon, Virginia 24210
Telephone (540) 628-3161

★

Carter House
301 L Street
Eureka, California 95501
Telephone (707) 445-1390

★

The Martine Inn
255 Oceanview Drive
Pacific Grove, California 93950
Telephone (408) 373-3388

Space Needle Restaurant
219 Fourth Avenue North
Seattle, Washington 98109
Telephone (206) 443-2100

★

The Golden Lamb Inn
27 South Broadway
Lebanon, Ohio 45036
Telephone (513) 932-5065

★

Eagle Ridge Inn & Resort
444 Eagle Ridge Drive
Galena, Illinois 61036
Telephone (815) 777-2444

★

Dos Casas Viejas
610 Agua Fria Street
Santa Fe, New Mexico 87501
Telephone (505) 983-1636

★

The Inn Above Onion Creek
4444 Highway 150
Kyle, Texas 78640
Telephone (512) 268-1617

Family reunions, birthdays and all of the holidays that your family looks forward to and celebrates each year come with their own unique traditions, feasts, get-togethers and gift-giving.

There are so many details to handle. So much to do! And, amid all the fun and flurry of activity, someone has to do the cooking! All the planning and preparation has to fit around everyday meals and the countless other details that are part of our busy lives.

To give you a helping hand, the home economists at Pillsbury and the American Dairy Association have gathered together favorite tips and preparation guidelines for making holidays and celebrations more fun and hassle free. We hope you find them as useful as we do.

And, beginning on page 58, you'll find a collection of Quick & Easy favorite recipes that are certain to make your entertaining easier — and those special occasions even more so!

Enjoy!

FESTIVE HOLIDAY DINNERS OR PARTIES

The focal point of so many celebrations is the food. No wonder we're willing to put so much time and effort into them!

Planning

The time you spend planning before a dinner or party will pay off the day of the event. This is the time to consider who will be coming, what you'll be serving, how and when you'll fit the preparation into your schedule, how much you will spend, and how you will serve the food.

Don't Tackle Too Much!

Be realistic about how much time you really have to get ready for the event. If you're pressed for time, consider a "bring your favorite hors d'oeuvre" party or a "planned-ahead potluck" where you supply guests with recipes to prepare and share. If necessary, enlist help; hire a friend or a college student or two to help with serving and clean-up.

Create the Menu

This is the fun part! Balance is the key so plan for...

- hot and cold
- spicy and mild
- sweet and savory
- a variety of colors
- a variety of textures
- a variety of shapes

A Workable Timetable

2 to 4 weeks ahead:
— Send out or call with invitations.

1 to 2 weeks ahead:
— Plan the menu.
— Write a detailed meal preparation schedule that notes what will be done in advance and what needs to be prepared the day of the event. Then plan the order of preparation.
— Make notes of special equipment, additional seating or serving pieces you'll need.
— Buy any paper goods and beverages.

3 to 5 days ahead:
— Check table coverings; clean and press them, if necessary.
— Decide what you'll wear and make sure that it's ready.
— If you're borrowing folding tables and chairs, round them up now.

3 days ahead:
— Check your pantry and refrigerator to make your shopping list. Then give yourself ample time to shop.

1 to 3 days ahead:
— Clean the house and clean or polish serving dishes.
— Prepare recipes that can be made ahead and refrigerate or freeze them. If necessary, arrange for additional storage at neighbors.

1 day ahead:
— Set up the beverage area, select music, arrange decorations and set up the feast table.
— Set out the serving dishes.

Day of party:
— Following your timetable, make the remaining recipes and add finishing touches to made-ahead recipes.
— Buy ice, flowers and other perishables.
— Take a final look at the house.
— Post a list of foods so you don't forget anything.
— Allow 1 hour to catch your breath, relax and get ready.

The Final Countdown

To ensure that everything is ready on time, prepare a schedule for the day of your dinner or party, listing everything you need to do in the order in which it needs to be done. Turn to pages 58 and 61 for schedules for traditional turkey and beef roast dinners.

◆ ◆ ◆ ◆ ◆ ◆ ◆ ◆ ◆ ◆ ◆ ◆ ◆ ◆ ◆ ◆ ◆ ◆ ◆ ◆

EVERYDAY MEAL SOLUTIONS

Preparing for major celebrations always cuts into the time we need for the preparation of everyday meals. To eliminate unnecessary trips to the store, make lists of the items you will need for meals.

Meal Planning Short Cuts

- Make it a family affair. Share menu planning and preparation with family members.
- Convenience foods. Once you have selected the main course, choose easy side dishes that will add color, variety, texture and nutrition to the meal.
- Double up. When you do find the time to cook, double the recipes and freeze the extra. You've just made two meals in the time it takes to make one! Be sure to wrap foods securely using airtight, moisture-proof wrap, freezer containers or plastic wrap.

Other Gatherings for Holiday Festivities

In addition to the holidays, graduations, anniversaries and family reunions are just a few of the occasions when you may be feeding a crowd. Unless you have a lot of tables and can arrange a wait staff, serving large groups is best accommodated with buffet service.

Open House Buffet

Foods must be easy to serve and easy to eat. Avoid dishes that require cutting with a knife and fork if guests will be balancing plates on their laps.

The number to serve and space available will determine where you place your buffet table and how many serving lines you'll have. Often beverages and/or desserts can be served away from the main buffet tables.

Arrange your buffet table so that it is easy for your guests. Begin with the plates, then the main course followed by other foods from hot to cold. If guests need two hands to serve themselves a food, such as salad, allow space for them to set down their plates. Flatware, napkins and beverages come last.

Add more drama and interest to your buffet by displaying dishes at different levels. Place pans or bowls upside down on the table, drape them with a tablecloth or napkins and arrange serving bowls and plates on top.

Potluck

Whether it's an open house or sit-down meal, a potluck menu is a fun and easy way to entertain. It minimizes planning and expenses for the host and allows the guests to share in the preparation. Here are a few things to keep in mind when selecting your potluck offering:

- Will there be time and room to do any final preparation after you arrive at your destination?
- Can your dish be served at room temperature? If not, how will you keep it hot or cold?
- Is your food easy to serve and eat?
- Does your dish travel well? Or does it require extra care to arrive in good condition?
- Will you need to bring containers and utensils for serving and eating?

Appetizer Trays

Party trays of cheeses, meats, fruits or vegetables to serve with crackers, small buns or dips are a welcome addition at almost any gathering.

- For a cheese appetizer tray, allow 1 1/2 ounces per person. Offer a selection of cheese flavors and textures. For greater visual appeal, cut cheeses in a variety of shapes, such as cubes, wedges, wheels, strips or slices.
- Meat can be sliced, rolled or cubed.
- Fruits can be cut in a variety of shapes. Plan 1/2 cup bite-size pieces for each serving.
- Vegetables can be prepared in advance and kept crisp in ice water until time to arrange on a tray. Drain them well.
- Moist foods should be served on their own tray or in a separate container to ensure that crackers and chips remain crisp and crunchy.
- Platters can be arranged ahead of time. Wrap well with plastic wrap and refrigerate. Remove cheese tray from the refrigerator at least 1/2 hour before serving but keep wrapped.
- For a more finished, professional look, garnish platters with sprigs of fresh herbs.

Accommodating Crowds

Don't be intimidated by the task of planning food for a crowd. To avoid lots of leftovers or worse, not enough food, multiply the individual serving size by the number of guests (or servings) you anticipate.

Average Serving Size

Appetizers	3 to 5 pieces (1/2 cup approx.)
Meat	2 to 3 oz.
Side Dishes	1/2 cup
Condiments	1 to 2 teaspoons (mustard, mayo, etc.)
Dips	1 tablespoon
Ice Cream	1/2 cup

Just a reminder: 16 ounces = 1 pound;
16 cups (32 1/2-cup portions) = 1 gallon.

Quick and Easy Favorites

From Across America

Traditional Turkey Dinner

(for 8 to 10)

Menu:

Savory Roast Turkey

Sausage Apple Stuffing

Savory Gravy

Hungry Jack® Mashed Potatoes

Shoepeg Corn with Basil Mustard

Early Peas with Honey Pecan Butter

Purchased Cranberry Sauce or Relish

Pillsbury Crescent Dinner Rolls

Maple Pecan Pumpkin Pie

What could be more satisfying than gathering family or friends for a tasty turkey dinner? A bit tricky, you say? Here is a menu of delicious foods with a timetable designed to help you with this feast.

Preparation Schedule for a Traditional Turkey Dinner for 8 to 10

Several days before dinner:
- If using a frozen turkey, refrigerate to thaw.
- Bake and cool Maple Pecan Pumpkin Pie; wrap and freeze without topping.

4 to 5 hours before dinner:
- Prepare Savory Roast Turkey.
- Prepare Sausage Apple Stuffing; stuff turkey and begin roasting.
- Remove pie from freezer; unwrap to thaw.

2 hours before dinner:
- For Early Peas with Honey Pecan Butter, combine ingredients for Honey Pecan Butter.
- For Shoepeg Corn with Basil Mustard, combine ingredients for Basil Mustard.

1 hour before dinner:
- Prepare Topping for Maple Pecan Pumpkin Pie; complete pie.
- Prepare Mashed Potatoes; keep warm in oven in oven-proof dish.

45 minutes before dinner:
- Remove Savory Roast Turkey when thermometer registers 180°F; remove from roasting pan and cover to keep warm.
- Prepare Savory Gravy; keep warm.

30 minutes before dinner:
- Complete preparation of Shoepeg Corn with Basil Mustard and Early Peas with Honey Pecan Butter.
- Bake Crescent Dinner Rolls.

15 minutes before dinner:
- Enlist help to pour ice water and light table candles.
- Slice roast turkey; place on warmed platter.
- Place all foods in serving dishes.

SAVORY ROAST TURKEY

Yield: 12 servings

- 1 (12 to 14-lb.) fresh or frozen whole turkey, thawed
- 1 to 2 tablespoons Aćcent® Flavor Enhancer
- ½ teaspoon salt
- ¼ teaspoon pepper
- ¼ cup (½ stick) butter, melted
- 1 tablespoon chopped fresh sage or 1 teaspoon dried sage leaves
- 1 tablespoon chopped fresh thyme or 1 teaspoon dried thyme leaves

Savory Roast Turkey
Sausage Apple Stuffing

Heat oven to 325°F. Remove giblets and neck from turkey. Rinse turkey inside and out with cold water, pat dry with paper towels. Place turkey, breast side up, on rack in shallow roasting pan.

In small bowl, combine flavor enhancer, salt and pepper; rub mixture on outside of turkey and inside cavity. Fill cavity with Sausage Apple Stuffing.

Combine butter, sage and thyme; brush half of mixture over turkey. Cover turkey with loose tent of foil.

Bake at 325°F for 15 minutes per pound (20 minutes per pound if stuffed), about 3 to 4 hours or until meat thermometer inserted into thickest part of thigh registers 180 to 185°F. To brown turkey, remove foil for last hour of baking. Baste turkey with remaining butter mixture. Juices should run clear when thigh is pierced with a fork and leg joint moves easily. Let turkey stand 15 minutes before carving.

Tip: Sage and thyme can be omitted. Baste with melted butter as directed above.

SAUSAGE APPLE STUFFING

Yield: 7 cups

- ¼ lb. bulk pork sausage
- ⅓ cup chopped onion
- ⅓ cup chopped celery
- 6 cups dry bread cubes
- 1 tablespoon finely chopped fresh parsley
- ¾ teaspoon Aćcent® Flavor Enhancer
- ¾ teaspoon salt
- 1½ teaspoons poultry seasoning
- ⅛ teaspoon pepper
- 3 tablespoons butter, melted
- ⅓ cup water
- 1½ cups chopped peeled apples
- ½ cup raisins
- Savory Roast Turkey

In small skillet, brown pork sausage with onion and celery; do not drain. In large bowl, combine bread cubes, parsley, flavor enhancer, salt, poultry seasoning, pepper and butter; mix well. Stir in water, apples, raisins and sausage mixture including drippings.

Prepare Savory Roasted Turkey as directed in recipe. Just before roasting, spoon stuffing into turkey; do not pack tightly.* Continue as directed in Savory Roast Turkey recipe.

TIP: *Stuffing will fill 18-lb. turkey. For smaller turkeys, the extra stuffing can be heated in slow-cooker. After stuffing turkey, measure remaining stuffing and spoon into slow-cooker; cover. Heat on high setting for 30 minutes; reduce heat setting to low. As turkey produces drippings, or after 2 hours, add 1 tablespoon drippings or chicken broth for each cup of stuffing in slow-cooker; mix lightly.

SAVORY TURKEY GRAVY

Yield: 3½ cups

- *Savory Roast Turkey drippings*
- 1 *(14½-oz.) can chicken broth*
- ⅓ *cup Pillsbury BEST® All Purpose Flour*
- *Water*

Prepare Savory Roast Turkey; remove from roasting pan. Pour drippings from pan into strainer over small bowl. Spoon off fat that rises to top, reserving 1/4 cup. Pour drippings into measuring cup. Add chicken broth and enough water to equal 3 1/2 cups liquid.

In medium saucepan, combine reserved 1/4 cup fat and flour. Cook over medium heat, stirring constantly with wire whisk until mixture turns golden brown, about 2 minutes. Gradually stir turkey drippings mixture into saucepan. Cook over low heat until mixture boils and thickens, stirring constantly.

TIP: Flour can be increased to 1/2 cup for thicker gravy.

EARLY PEAS WITH HONEY PECAN BUTTER

Yield: 10 servings

- 2 *(15-oz.) cans LeSueur® Very Young Small Early Peas*
- 2 *tablespoons butter*
- 2 to 4 *tablespoons honey*
- 6 *tablespoons coarsely chopped pecans*

In medium saucepan, heat peas; drain well. Meanwhile in small saucepan, melt butter; stir in honey and pecans. Pour over peas; stir to blend.

SHOEPEG CORN WITH BASIL MUSTARD

Yield: 10 servings

- 3 *(11-oz.) cans Green Giant® White Shoepeg or Sweet Select® Yellow and White Corn*
- 2 *tablespoons butter, softened*
- 2 *tablespoons Dijon mustard*
- 8 *teaspoons chopped fresh basil or 1 teaspoon dried basil leaves*

In medium saucepan, heat corn; drain well. In small bowl, combine remaining ingredients; mix well. Stir into corn. If desired, salt and pepper to taste.

MAPLE PECAN PUMPKIN PIE

Yield: 10 servings

- 1 *(15-oz.) pkg. Pillsbury Refrigerated Pie Crusts*

Filling:

- ½ *cup sugar*
- 1 *teaspoon cinnamon*
- ½ *teaspoon salt*
- ¼ *cup raisins*
- ¼ *cup chopped pecans*
- 1 *(16-oz.) can (2 cups) pumpkin*
- 1 *(12-oz.) can (1½ cups) PET® Evaporated Milk*
- 1 *teaspoon maple extract*
- 2 *eggs, slightly beaten*

Topping:

- 1½ *cups whipping cream*
- ¼ *cup powdered sugar*
- ½ *teaspoon maple extract*
- *Pecan halves*

Prepare pie crust according to package directions for one-crust filled pie using 9-inch pie pan. (Refrigerate remaining crust for a later use.)

Heat oven to 425°F. In large bowl, combine all filling ingredients; blend well. Pour into crust-lined pan. Bake at 425°F for 15 minutes. Reduce oven temperature to 350°F; bake an additional 40 to 45 minutes or until knife inserted near center comes out clean. Cover edge of crust with strips of foil after 15 to 20 minutes of baking to prevent excessive browning. Cool completely.

In small bowl, beat whipping cream until soft peaks form. Add powdered sugar and maple extract; beat until stiff peaks form. Spread over cooled pie. Refrigerate until serving time. If desired, garnish with pecan halves.

◆ ◆ ◆ ◆ ◆ ◆ ◆ ◆ ◆ ◆

Timetable for Roasting Poultry

(Oven Temperature 325°F
Thermometer Reading 180°F to 185°F)

Poultry	Weight In Pounds	Total Roasting Time In Hours
Chicken (stuffed)	2½ to 4½	2 to 3½
Capon (stuffed)	4 to 8	2½ to 4½
Turkey (stuffed)	4 to 6	2 to 3
	6 to 8	3 to 3½
	8 to 12	3½ to 4½
	12 to 16	4½ to 5½
	16 to 18	5½ to 6½
	20 to 24	6½ to 7
	24 to 28	7½ to 8
Cornish Game Hen* (stuffed or unstuffed)	1 to 1½	1 to 2
Duck (stuffed)**	3 to 5	2 to 3
Goose (stuffed)**	4 to 8	2¾ to 3½
	8 to 14	3½ to 5

* Roast at 350°F.
** Roast at 400°F for 15 minutes, then at 325°F.

◆ ◆ ◆ ◆ ◆ ◆ ◆ ◆ ◆ ◆

TRADITIONAL BEEF ROAST DINNER

(FOR 8 TO 12)

Menu:

Boneless Beef Roast with Horseradish Sauce

Cheddar Potatoes with Wreath of Vegetables

Asparagus Spears with Mushroom-Almond Topping

Jicama Spinach Salad

Pillsbury Crescent Dinner Rolls

Macadamia Fudge Torte

♦ ♦ ♦ ♦ ♦ ♦ ♦ ♦ ♦ ♦ ♦ ♦ ♦ ♦

*F*or a festive Christmas dinner that is easy to make and a feast for the eyes as well, we are suggesting a delicious juicy roast beef. The vegetable dishes will brighten the table, and to lighten the feast day preparations, the dessert can be waiting in the freezer.

Preparation Schedule for a Traditional Beef Rib Roast Dinner for 8 to 10

Morning of dinner:

— Bake Macadamia Fudge Torte or remove from freezer to thaw if already prepared.
— Cut out jicama shapes and prepare dressing for Jicama Spinach Salad.
— Set table; arrange flowers and other finishing touches to the house.

4 hours before dinner:

— Prepare potato mixture for Cheddar Potatoes with Wreath of Vegetables; cover and refrigerate.

2 to 4 hours before dinner:

— Place beef roast in oven depending on desired degree of doneness.

2 hours before dinner:

— Combine spinach, strawberries and jicama in salad bowl for Jicama Spinach Salad; cover and refrigerate.
— Prepare Horseradish Sauce.

1 hour before dinner:

— Assemble ingredients for Asparagus Spears with Mushroom-Almond Topping.

45 minutes before dinner:

— Place potato mixture for Cheddar Potatoes with Wreath of Vegetables in oven.
— Remove beef roast at desired doneness; cover tightly to keep warm.

30 minutes before dinner:

— Complete preparation of Asparagus Spears with Mushroom-Almond Topping.
— Bake Crescent Dinner Rolls.
— Cook vegetables and complete assembly of Cheddar Potatoes with Wreath of Vegetables.

15 minutes before dinner:

— Enlist help to pour ice water and light table candles.
— Make AuJus Gravy, if desired.
— Slice beef roast; place on warmed platter.
— Toss dressing with spinach mixture for Jicama Spinach Salad.
— Place all foods in serving dishes.

Boneless Beef Roast
Jicama Spinach Salad
Cheddar Potatoes with Wreath of Vegetables

CHEDDAR POTATOES WITH WREATH OF VEGETABLES

Yield: 10 servings

- *1½ cups water*
- *2 tablespoons butter*
- *⅛ teaspoon garlic powder*
- *⅛ teaspoon pepper*
- *3 cups Hungry Jack® Mashed Potato Flakes*
- *1 cup milk*
- *4 ounces (1 cup) shredded Cheddar cheese*
- *2 teaspoons prepared mustard*
- *2 eggs, slightly beaten*
- *2 (8-oz.) pkg. Green Giant® Harvest Fresh® Frozen Broccoli, Cauliflower and Carrots*
- *2 tablespoons butter*

Heat oven to 325°F. Lightly butter 2-quart casserole. In medium saucepan, bring water, 2 tablespoons butter, garlic powder and pepper to a boil. Remove from heat; stir in potato flakes, milk, cheese, mustard and eggs until well blended. Place potato mixture in buttered casserole. Using back of spoon, make indentation in potato mixture around edge of casserole 2 inches wide by 1 inch deep.* Bake uncovered at 325°F for 20 to 25 minutes or until thoroughly heated.

Meanwhile, cook vegetables according to package directions; drain. Add 2 tablespoons butter; stir to coat. Spoon cooked vegetables into indented ring in hot potato mixture.

TIP: *To make ahead, prepare potatoes to this point. Cover; refrigerate up to 24 hours. Bake uncovered at 325°F for 30 to 35 minutes or until thoroughly heated. Continue as directed above.

BONELESS BEEF ROAST

Yield: 8 to 10 servings

4 to 6 pounds boneless beef roast

Heat oven to 325°F. If desired, sprinkle roast with salt and pepper. Place fat side up on rack in shallow roasting pan. Insert meat thermometer so bulb reaches center of thickest part of meat but does not rest in fat. Roast at 325°F for 2 to 4 hours or until desired degree of doneness. Roast to 140°F for rare meat, 160°F for medium and 170°F for well done meat.

For ease in carving, let roast stand covered 10 to 15 minutes to set juices.

TIP: For Aujus Gravy, after removing roast from pan, skim off fat from meat juice. Add 1/3 to 1/2 cup water. Bring to a boil, stirring and scraping pan. Season to taste. If desired, strain; serve with meat.

HORSERADISH SAUCE

Yield: 1 cup

In small bowl, beat 1/2 cup whipping cream, 1/4 teaspoon each salt and dry mustard and dash of pepper until soft peaks form. Fold in 3 tablespoons horseradish. Store covered in refrigerator.

ASPARAGUS SPEARS WITH MUSHROOM-ALMOND TOPPING

Yield: 10 servings

- *3 (15-oz.) cans Green Giant® Extra Long Tender Green Asparagus Spears, undrained*
- *¼ cup (½ stick) butter*
- *1 (4.5-oz.) jar Green Giant® Sliced Mushrooms, drained*
- *¼ cup slivered almonds*
- *1 teaspoon dried basil leaves*
- *¼ teaspoon pepper*

In large skillet, heat asparagus; drain. In small saucepan, combine butter, mushrooms, almonds, basil and pepper; heat thoroughly. Remove spears from skillet with spatula. Place on warm serving platter. Pour mushroom mixture over spears. Serve immediately.

JICAMA SPINACH SALAD

Yield: 8 to 10 servings

Peel 1 jicama; cut into 1/4-inch slices. Using canape cutters, cut desired shapes from slices. In large bowl, combine 10-oz. fresh spinach, 1 cup sliced strawberries or seeds of 1 pomegranate and jicama cutouts; cover and refrigerate. In small jar with tight-fitting lid; combine 1/4 cup lime juice, 3 tablespoons honey and 2 tablespoons oil; shake well and refrigerate. At serving time, toss salad with dressing.

◆ ◆ ◆ ◆ ◆ ◆ ◆ ◆ ◆ ◆

Timetable for Roasting Beef

(Oven Temperature 325°F)

Roast	Weight In Pounds	Thermometer Reading (°F)	Cooking Time* (Minutes Per Pound)
Rib (Bone in)	6 to 8	140°F (rare) 160°F (med.) 170°F (well)	23 to 25 27 to 30 32 to 35
Boneless or Rolled Rib	4 to 6	140°F (rare) 160°F (med.) 170°F (well)	26 to 32 34 to 38 40 to 42
Rib Eye**	4 to 6	140°F (rare) 160°F (med.) 170°F (well)	18 to 20 20 to 22 22 to 24
Boneless or Rolled Rump	4 to 6	150°F to 170°F	25 to 30
Sirloin Tip	3½ to 4 6 to 8	140°F to 170°F 140°F to 170°F	35 to 40 30 to 35
Top Round	4 to 6	140°F to 170°F	25 to 30

* Based on meat taken directly from refrigerator.
** Roast at 350°F.

◆ ◆ ◆ ◆ ◆ ◆ ◆ ◆ ◆ ◆

MACADAMIA FUDGE TORTE

Yield: 12 servings

Filling

- ⅓ *cup low-fat sweetened condensed milk (not evaporated)*
- ½ *cup semi-sweet chocolate chips*

Cake

- 1 *pkg. Pillsbury Moist Supreme® Devil's Food Cake Mix*
- 1½ *teaspoons cinnamon*
- ⅓ *cup oil*
- 1 *(16-oz.) can sliced pears in light syrup, drained*
- 2 *eggs*
- ⅓ *cup chopped macadamia nuts or pecans*
- 2 *teaspoons water*

Sauce

- 1 *(17-oz.) jar butterscotch caramel fudge ice cream topping*
- ⅓ *cup milk*

Haagen-Dazs® Vanilla Ice Cream or Frozen Yogurt

Heat oven to 350°F. Butter 9 or 10-inch springform pan. In small saucepan, combine filling ingredients. Cook over medium-low heat until chocolate is melted, stirring occasionally.

In large bowl, combine cake mix, cinnamon and oil; blend at low speed for 20 to 30 seconds or until crumbly. (Mixture will be dry.) Place pears in blender container or food processor bowl with metal blade; cover and blend until smooth.

In large bowl, combine 2 1/2 cups of the cake mix mixture, pureed pears and eggs; beat at low speed until moistened. Beat 2 minutes at medium speed. Spread batter evenly in buttered pan. Drop filling by spoonfuls over batter. Stir nuts and water into remaining cake mix mixture. Sprinkle over filling.

Bake at 350°F for 45 to 50 minutes or until top springs back when touched lightly in center. Cool 10 minutes. Remove sides of pan. Cool 1 1/2 hours or until completely cooled.

In small saucepan, combine sauce ingredients. Cook over medium-low heat for 3 to 4 minutes or until well blended, stirring occasionally. To serve, spoon 2 tablespoons warm sauce onto each serving plate; top with wedge of torte and scoop of ice cream. If desired, garnish with chocolate curls.

FIESTA OPEN HOUSE (FOR 8 TO 12)

Menu:

Choose two of the following appetizers:
Mexican Snack Squares
Salsa and Sour Cream Dip
Southwestern Black Bean Salsa
Chile and Cheese Appetizer Tart

White Turkey Chili
Salsa Bread Olé

Sugar-Crusted Almond Pastries

Beverages of your choice

◆ ◆ ◆ ◆ ◆ ◆ ◆ ◆ ◆ ◆ ◆ ◆ ◆

Recipes with lively colors and flavors highlight this menu and offer a theme for your party. Choose it for a festive holiday gathering or for sports fans as they gather around your TV. If you are having a party for more than 8 to 12, make all of the appetizers and increase the chili recipe. Most of the recipes can be easily transported for those who offer to bring something and the chili makes delicious use of turkey that may be left-over from a holiday bird.

MEXICAN SNACK SQUARES

Yield: 48 squares

- 2 *(8-oz.) cans Pillsbury Refrigerated Crescent Dinner Rolls*
- 1 *(16-oz.) can Old El Paso® Refried Beans*
- 1 *cup sour cream*
- 2 *tablespoons Old El Paso® Taco Seasoning mix (from 1¼-oz. pkg.)*
- 6 *ounces (1½ cups) shredded Cheddar cheese*
- ½ *cup sliced green onions*
- ½ *cup chopped green bell pepper*
- 1 *cup seeded, chopped tomatoes*
- ½ *cup sliced ripe olives*

Mexican Snack Squares

Heat oven to 375°F. Separate dough into 4 long rectangles. Place cross-wise in ungreased 15x10x1-inch baking pan; press over bottom and 1 inch up sides to form crust. Firmly press perforations to seal. Bake at 375°F for 14 to 19 minutes or until golden brown. Cool completely.

Spread beans over crust to within 1/2 inch of edges. In small bowl, combine sour cream and taco seasoning mix; mix well. Spread sour cream mixture over beans. Sprinkle cheese, onions, bell pepper, tomatoes and olives evenly over sour cream mixture. Cover; refrigerate 1 hour. Cut into squares. Serve with salsa, if desired.

Chile and Cheese Appetizer Tart

SALSA AND SOUR CREAM DIP

Yield: 3 cups

- 1 *(16-oz.) container sour cream*
- 1 *cup Old El Paso® Homestyle Salsa with Garden Peppers or Thick 'N Chunky Salsa*
- 1 *(1¼-oz.) envelope Old El Paso® 40% Less Sodium Taco Seasoning Mix or regular Taco Seasoning Mix*

Combine all ingredients in 1-quart bowl; mix well. Cover; refrigerate. Serve with tortilla chips.

SOUTHWESTERN BLACK BEAN SALSA

Yield: 5 cups

- 2 *(16-oz.) jars Old El Paso® Mild or Medium Thick 'n Chunky Picante*
- ½ *teaspoon sugar*
- 1 *tablespoon fresh lime juice*
- ⅓ *cup chopped green onions, including tops*
- ⅓ *cup chopped red onion*
- ⅓ *cup finely chopped fresh cilantro*
- 1 *(11-oz.) can Green Giant® Mexicorn® Whole Kernel Corn, Red and Green Peppers*
- 1 *(15-oz.) can Green Giant®, Joan of Arc® or Progresso® Black Beans, drained, rinsed*

In large bowl, combine picante, sugar and lime juice; mix well. Add all remaining ingredients; stir gently. Cover; refrigerate at least 1 hour. Serve with tortilla chips.

CHILE & CHEESE APPETIZER TART

Yield: 16 servings

- 1 *(15-oz.) pkg. Pillsbury Refrigerated Pie Crusts*
- 4 *ounces (1 cup) shredded Cheddar cheese*
- 4 *ounces (1 cup) shredded Monterey Jack cheese*
- 1 *(4-oz.) can Old El Paso® Chopped Green Chiles, drained*
- ¼ *teaspoon chili powder*
- 1 *cup Old El Paso® Thick 'N Chunky Salsa*

Allow both crust pouches to stand at room temperature for 15 to 20 minutes. Heat oven to 450°F. Unfold one crust onto ungreased cookie sheet; remove plastic sheet and press out fold lines. Sprinkle cheeses over crust to within 1/2 inch of edge; sprinkle with green chilies. Unfold remaining crust, remove plastic sheets and press out fold lines. Place over chilies. Seal edges with fork; generously prick top crust with fork. Sprinkle with chili powder.

Bake at 450°F for 10 to 15 minutes or until golden brown. Let stand 5 minutes. Cut into wedges. Serve with salsa.

◆ ◆ ◆ ◆ ◆ ◆ ◆ ◆ ◆ ◆

Simple Touches for Festive Flair

— Garnish foods with fresh herbs. Fresh rosemary sprigs and cranberries placed to resemble holly add a festive touch to a holiday meat platter.

— Accent each place setting with a holiday-shaped votive candle.

— Set an ornament tied with a bow at each place setting as a gift for the guest.

— Create place cards, writing with a silver or gold pen, on special items, such as ornaments or Easter eggs.

— Tie gold ribbon around the stems of wine glasses.

— Gather together fabric at each corner and tie with flowers and a bright ribbon.

— Use paper and plastic holiday table items for convenience. Tie plastic silverware together with festive ribbon.

— Create a stunning centerpiece by mixing and matching silver and crystal candleholders from your collection. Use a variety of gilded tapers, pillars and sphere-shaped candles for added interest.

◆ ◆ ◆ ◆ ◆ ◆ ◆ ◆ ◆ ◆

White Turkey Chili

Salsa Bread Olé

Yield: 1 (24-slice) loaf

- 3 *eggs*
- ½ *cup cornmeal*
- ⅔ *cup buttermilk*
- ½ *cup (1 stick) butter, softened*
- 1 *(16-oz.) jar Old El Paso® Mild Thick 'N Chunky Salsa or Picante, well drained*
- ½ *cup chopped ripe olives*
- ¼ *cup chopped scallions or green onions*
- 1 *tablespoon chopped fresh parsley*
- 5 *ounces (1¼ cups) shredded Cheddar cheese*
- 1 *ounce (¼ cup) shredded Monterey Jack cheese, if desired*
- 2 *cups Pillsbury BEST® All Purpose Flour*
- 1 *cup Hungry Jack® Mashed Potato Flakes*
- 4 *teaspoons Old El Paso® Taco Seasoning Mix*
- 3 *teaspoons baking powder*
- 1 *teaspoon baking soda*
- ¼ *teaspoon salt*
- ¼ *teaspoon pepper*

Heat oven to 350°F. Butter and flour 10-inch tube or 12-cup Bundt® pan. In large bowl, beat eggs at high speed for 1 minute. Add cornmeal, buttermilk, butter and salsa. Beat 1 minute at medium speed or until well blended. With spoon, stir in olives, scallions, parsley and cheeses. Lightly spoon flour into measuring cup; level off. In medium bowl, combine flour and all remaining ingredients; mix well. Add to salsa mixture. Stir until well blended. Spoon batter into buttered and floured pan.

Bake at 350°F for 45 to 50 minutes or until toothpick inserted in center comes out clean. Cool 15 minutes. Remove from pan. Cool 20 minutes. Serve warm.

White Turkey Chili

Yield: 12 (1 cup) servings

- 2 *tablespoons butter*
- 1 *cup chopped onion*
- 2 *ribs celery, thinly sliced*
- 4 *cups chopped cooked turkey*
- 2 *(15.5-oz.) cans Green Giant® Great Northern Beans, drained*
- 2 *(14.5-oz.) cans ready-to-serve chicken broth*
- 2 *(11-oz.) cans Green Giant® White Shoepeg Corn*
- 2 *(4-oz.) cans Old El Paso® Chopped Green Chiles*
- 4 *teaspoons cumin*
- ½ *teaspoon hot pepper sauce, if desired*
- 4 *ounces (1 cup) shredded Monterey Jack cheese*
- 2 *tablespoons chopped fresh parsley*

Heat butter in large saucepan over medium heat until hot. Add onion and celery; cook and stir 2 to 3 minutes or until vegetables are tender. Stir in remaining ingredients except cheese and parsley; blend well. Cover and cook 15 to 20 minutes or until thoroughly heated, stirring occasionally. To serve, ladle chili into bowls; sprinkle with cheese and parsley.

Sugar-Crusted Almond Pastries

Yield: 24 pastries

- 2 *(8-oz.) cans Pillsbury Refrigerated Crescent Dinner Rolls*
- ½ *cup (1 stick) butter*
- 2 *cups slivered almonds*
- 1⅓ *cups sugar*

Heat oven to 375°F. Unroll dough into 2 large rectangles. Place in ungreased 15x10x1-inch baking pan; press over bottom to form crust. Seal perforations. Melt butter in medium saucepan over low heat. Cook and stir 4 to 5 minutes or until light golden brown. Add almonds and sugar; stir to coat. Spoon and spread mixture evenly over dough.

Bake at 375°F for 11 to 16 minutes or until crust is deep golden brown. Cool 30 minutes. Cut into squares. Serve warm or cool.

COOKIES 'N CONFECTIONS

Cookies, candies, breads or cakes! So easy to make and festive indeed! Your homebaked gifts can be creatively given in decorative tins lined with bright tissue or festive bags tied with colorful ribbon. Whatever the occasion, mouthwatering homemade treats are always appreciated.

♦ ♦

FROSTED SUGAR COOKIES

Start with Pillsbury Refrigerated Sugar Cookie Dough and your favorite cookie cutters. Follow directions on the package for rolled cookies. Bake time will vary according to cookie size. To decorate unbaked cookies, sprinkle with colored decorator sugars or candy sprinkles before baking. To decorate baked cookies with frosting, place frosting in heavy resealable plastic sandwich bag. Cut small hole in one corner; close top and squeeze frosting gently through hole to make thin lines.

♦ ♦ ♦ ♦ ♦ ♦ ♦ ♦ ♦ ♦ ♦ ♦

To freeze cookies, cool them completely. Package each variety by itself in airtight, moisture-proof wrap, freezer containers or plastic bags. Unfrosted cookies can be frozen up to 12 months. Frosted cookies can be frozen one to two months. Freeze frosted cookies uncovered on a cookie sheet to set the frosting, then place them between layers of waxed paper in a rigid container. Wrap the container in a freezer-proof outer wrap. Remove frosted cookies from container to thaw.

♦ ♦ ♦ ♦ ♦ ♦ ♦ ♦ ♦ ♦ ♦ ♦

(Cookies appear clockwise)
Fruit Filled Cookies
Frosted Sugar Cookies
Quick Peanut Blossoms

FRUIT FILLED COOKIES

Yield: 2 dozen

- *1 (20-oz.) pkg. Pillsbury Refrigerated Sugar Cookies*
- *¼ cup raspberry jam or jelly*

Heat oven to 350°F. Slice dough into 24 (1/8-inch) slices. Refrigerate remaining dough. Place slices 2 inches apart on ungreased cookie sheets. Spread each slice with 1/2 teaspoon of jam to within 1/4 inch of edge. Set aside.

Slice remaining dough into 24 (1/4-inch) slices. Cut 1-inch star shape out of center of each cookie slice.* Place cookie slices on jam-topped cookie slices; press edges slightly. Bake at 350°F for 10 to 14 minutes or until edges are light golden brown. Cool 1 minute; remove from cookie sheets. Cool completely.

<u>TIP</u>: *To bake tiny stars from center of cookies, place on cookie sheet and bake 350°F for 4 to 6 minutes.

(Cookies appear clockwise)
Holiday Truffles
Dipped Chocolate Chip Cookies
Fruit Filled Cookies

PINEAPPLE CARROT QUICK BREAD

Yield: 1 (12-slice) loaf

Bread

- 1 *pkg. Pillsbury Carrot Quick Bread Mix*
- 1 *(8-oz.) can crushed pineapple in unsweetened juice, undrained*
- ¾ *cup water*
- ¼ *cup oil*
- 2 *eggs*

Glaze

- ½ *cup Pillsbury Creamy Supreme® Cream Cheese Frosting*

Heat oven to 350°F. Grease and flour bottom only of 8x4 or 9x5-inch loaf pan.

In large bowl, combine all bread ingredients. Stir 50 to 75 strokes by hand until dry particles are moistened. Pour batter into greased and floured pan.

Bake at 350°F for 60 to 70 minutes or until toothpick inserted in center comes out clean. Cool 15 minutes; remove from pan. Cool completely. Wrap tightly; store in refrigerator.

Just before serving, heat frosting in small saucepan over low heat just until it begins to melt. Remove from heat; stir. Drizzle over bread. Let stand until set. Store in refrigerator.

HIGH ALTITUDE - Above 3500 feet; Add 1/4 cup flour to quick bread mix. Bake at 375°F. for 40 to 50 minutes.

HOLIDAY TRUFFLES

Yield: 6 dozen candies

- 1 *(12-oz.) pkg. (2 cups) semi-sweet chocolate chips*
- ¼ *cup orange-flavored liqueur or 1 teaspoon orange extract*
- 1 *can Pillsbury Creamy Supreme® Chocolate Fudge or Chocolate Frosting*
- *Coconut, chocolate sprinkles, ground nuts or cocoa*

Melt chocolate chips in medium saucepan over low heat, stirring constantly; remove from heat. Stir in orange liqueur and frosting; blend well. Refrigerate 1 to 2 hours or until firm.

Place coconut in pie pan. Scoop mixture into 1-inch balls; drop onto coconut, (Mixture will be sticky.) Roll to coat. Place in foil candy cups, if desired. Store in refrigerator.

DIPPED CHOCOLATE CHIP COOKIES

Yield: 3 dozen cookies

- 1 *(20-oz.) pkg. Pillsbury Refrigerated Chocolate Chip or M&M's® Candies Cookies*
- 1 *cup semi-sweet chocolate chips*
- 1 *tablespoon shortening*

Heat oven to 350°F. Bake cookies as directed on package. Cool completely. In small saucepan over low heat, melt chocolate chips and shortening, stirring constantly. Dip half of each cookie into melted chocolate. Place on cookie sheet lined with wax paper. Refrigerate until chocolate is set.

QUICK PEANUT BLOSSOMS

Yield: 3 dozen cookies

- 1 *(20-oz.) pkg. Pillsbury Refrigerated Cookies with Skippy® Peanut Butter*
- 3 *tablespoons sugar*
- 36 *milk chocolate candy kisses*

Heat oven to 375°F. Shape dough into 1-inch balls; roll in sugar. Place 2 inches apart on ungreased cookie sheets.

Bake at 375°F for 10 to 12 minutes or until golden brown. Immediately top each cookie with 1 candy kiss, pressing down firmly so cookie cracks around edge. Remove from cookie sheets. Cool completely.

Chocolate Mint Cream Cake

Chocolate Mint Cream Cake

Yield: 12 servings

Cake
- 1 pkg. Pillsbury Moist Supreme® Devil's Food Cake Mix
- 1 cup water
- ½ cup (1 stick) butter, softened
- ¼ cup creme de menthe liqueur or syrup
- 3 eggs

Frosting
- 1 can Pillsbury Creamy Supreme® Vanilla Frosting
- 1 teaspoon mint extract, if desired
- 8 to 10 foil wrapped rectangular mints

Heat oven to 350°F. Butter and flour two 8 or 9-inch round cake pans. In large bowl, combine all cake ingredients at low speed until moistened; beat 2 minutes at medium speed. Pour batter into buttered and floured pans.

Bake at 350°F for 35 to 45 minutes or until toothpick inserted in center comes out clean. Cool 15 minutes; remove from pans. Cool completely.

In small bowl, combine frosting and mint extract; stir until blended. To assemble cake, spread frosting between cake layers: frost sides and top. To decorate with mint trees, unwrap mints. Cut 7 mints in half diagonally. Position triangular mint pieces side by side to create tree shape. Small squares can be cut from remaining mints to form tree trunks.

HIGH ALTITUDE - Above 3500 feet: Increase water to 1 cup plus 4 teaspoons and add 1/4 cup flour to cake mix. Bake at 375°F for 30 to 40 minutes in two 9-inch round cake pans.

Decadent Chocolate Cherry Bread

Yield: 16 servings

Bread
- 1 pkg. Pillsbury Nut or Date Quick Bread Mix
- 1 cup coarsely chopped pecans
- 1 (10-oz.) jar maraschino cherries, drained and cut in half, reserving liquid
- ¾ cup miniature semi-sweet chocolate chips
- ¾ cup water
- ¼ cup kirsch (cherry-flavored liqueur)*
- 1 tablespoon butter, melted
- 1 egg

Glaze
- ½ cup powdered sugar
- 1 tablespoon butter, softened
- 1 to 2 tablespoons reserved cherry liquid

Heat oven to 350°F. Butter and flour bottom only of 8x4 or 9x5-inch loaf pan.** In large bowl, combine all bread ingredients. Stir 50 to 75 strokes by hand until dry particles are moistened. Pour into buttered and floured pan.

Bake at 350°F for 65 to 80 minutes for 8x4-inch pan, 60 to 70 minutes for 9x5-inch pan, or until toothpick inserted in center comes out clean. Cool 15 minutes; remove from pan. Cool completely.

In small bowl, blend all glaze ingredients until smooth, adding enough cherry liquid for desired spreading consistency. Frost bread; if desired, decorate with additional cherries and nuts. Refrigerate until glaze is set. Wrap in plastic wrap or foil; store in refrigerator up to 2 weeks or freeze up to 3 months. For optimum flavor, refrigerate at least 24 hours before serving.

TIPS: *Two teaspoons almond extract plus 1/4 cup water can be substituted for 1/4 cup kirsch.

**Three 3x5-inch loaf pans can also be used. Bake at 350°F for 40 to 50 minutes.

HIGH ALTITUDE - Above 3500 feet: Add 1/4 cup flour to dry quick bread mix. Bake as directed above

Pillsbury Cinnamon Streusel Coffee Cake

Yield: 12 servings

This is a most versatile cake mix. It is delicious served as a coffee cake for breakfast or brunch, as a dessert or a coffee time treat! It is so easily made according to package directions and while it is baking, you have time for other meal preparations or activities.

Quick Apple Cranberry Pear Muffins

APPLE RICOTTA BRUNCH BISCUITS

Yield: 8 biscuits

- ½ *cup sugar*
- 1 *cup Ricotta cheese*
- 1 *egg*
- ¼ *cup sliced almonds*
- ½ *teaspoon cinnamon*
- 1 *(17.3-oz.) can Pillsbury GRANDS!® Refrigerated Buttermilk Biscuits*
- 1 *small apple, peeled, cut into 8 wedges (½ inch thick)*

Heat oven to 375°F. Spray 8 jumbo muffin cups or 8 (6-oz.) custard cups with nonstick cooking spray. In small bowl, combine sugar, cheese and egg; beat at high speed for 1 minute. In small bowl, combine almonds and cinnamon; mix well. Separate dough into 8 biscuits. Press each biscuit evenly in bottom and up sides of sprayed muffin cups. Place 1 wedge of apple in each cup. Spoon 2 rounded tablespoonfuls cheese mixture over each apple wedge; sprinkle with almond mixture.

Bake at 375°F for 20 to 25 minutes or until biscuits are deep golden brown and apples are crisp-tender. Remove biscuits from muffin cups; cool 15 minutes. Serve warm. Store in refrigerator.

PILLSBURY GRANDS!® SWEET ROLLS

Yield: 5 rolls

Fresh-baked rolls are hot and ready in just minutes prepared according to package directions. These giant swirls topped with creamy icing will delight family or friends for everyday or on special occasions.

QUICK APPLE CRANBERRY PEAR MUFFINS

Yield: 18 muffins

- 1 *pkg. Pillsbury Apple Cinnamon or Date Quick Bread Mix*
- ¾ *cup buttermilk**
- 3 *tablespoons oil*
- 1 *egg*
- 1 *cup fresh or frozen cranberries, thawed*
- ¾ *cup coarsely chopped walnuts*
- 1 *large firm pear, peeled, cut into ½-inch pieces*

Heat oven to 400°F. Line with paper baking cups or grease 18 muffin cups. In large bowl, combine quick bread mix, buttermilk, oil and egg. Stir 50 to 75 strokes with spoon until mix is moistened. Stir in cranberries, walnuts and pear. Spoon batter into paper-lined muffin cups. (Cups will be full.)

Bake at 400°F for 18 to 25 minutes or until golden brown. Serve warm or cool.

TIP: *To substitute for buttermilk, use 2 teaspoons vinegar or lemon juice plus milk to make 3/4 cup.

HIGH ALTITUDE - Above 3500 feet; Add 1/4 cup flour to quick bread mix. Bake as directed above.

ICED CINNAMON ROLL COFFEE CAKE

Yield: 6 to 8 servings

- 2 *tablespoons butter, softened*
- ¼ *cup sugar*
- 1 *teaspoon cinnamon*
- ¼ *cup finely chopped nuts*
- 1 *(12.4-oz.) can Pillsbury Refrigerated Cinnamon Rolls with Icing*

Heat oven to 375°F. Using 1 tablespoon of the butter, butter 9-inch pie pan. Combine sugar and cinnamon; sprinkle 2 tablespoons of the mixture over buttered pan. Sprinkle 3 tablespoons of the nuts over sugar mixture.

Separate dough into 8 rolls; cut each into quarters. Place half of pieces evenly over nuts; sprinkle with 1 tablespoon of the sugar mixture. Dot with remaining tablespoon butter; top with remaining dough pieces and sugar mixture.

Bake at 375°F for 18 to 20 minutes or until golden brown. Drizzle icing over rolls; sprinkle with remaining nuts. Cut into wedges. Serve warm.

EVERYDAY MEAL SOLUTIONS

Monday — Soup and Hot Bread
Tuesday — Skillet Meal
Wednesday — Hot Sandwich and Salad
Thursday — One-Dish or Casserole
Friday — Family Night Out
Saturday — Stovetop or Stir-Fry
Sunday — Brunch

What's for Dinner? Whether holiday time or any time, dinner is an everyday challenge. The formula or guide as stated above can be adapted to meet your needs for timely and tasty meals.

Here is an example of a week of meals using this guide and the recipe selections on these pages:

Monday - Tuna Pasta Primavera Soup (page 72) or Speedy Sausage 'N Lentil Soup (page 71) served with Onion Pepper Biscuits (page 72).

Tuesday - Taco and Black Bean Skillet Dinner or Sausage and Pasta Skillet (page 74).

Wednesday - Cheese Steak Crescent Braid (page 72), Fiesta Style Sloppy Joes! (page 73) or Ham and Cheese Crescent Pockets (page 72) and crispy garden salad.

Thursday - Vegetable Topped Microwave-Baked Potatoes (page 73) or Green Bean and Turkey Casserole (page 74).

Friday - Family Night Out.

Saturday - Szechuan Pork and Pasta Stir-fry (page 73).

Sunday - Chicken and Pasta in Cajun Cream (page 73).

SPEEDY SAUSAGE 'N LENTIL SOUP

Yield: 3 servings

- *1 tablespoon butter*
- *¼ cup chopped onion*
- *1 celery stalk, sliced*
- *1 medium carrot, sliced*
- *2 small red potatoes, cut into chunks*
- *1 smoked cooked sausage, cut into chunks*
- *1 (19-oz.) can Progresso® Lentil Soup*

In medium saucepan, melt butter over medium-high heat; add onion, celery, carrots and potatoes. Cook and stir 5 minutes. Add sausage and soup; bring to a boil. Reduce heat; cover and simmer 15 to 20 minutes or until vegetables are tender.

Speedy Sausage 'N Lentil Soup
Onion Pepper Biscuits

Cheese Steak Crescent Braid

Onion Pepper Biscuits

Yield: 8 servings

- 1 *(17.3-oz.) can GRANDS!® Refrigerated Buttermilk Biscuits*
- 3 *tablespoons finely chopped onion*
- 1 *tablespoon butter*
- ¼ to ½ *teaspoon coarsely ground black pepper*

Heat oven to 375°F. Separate dough into 8 biscuits; place on unbuttered cookie sheet. In small saucepan over medium heat, cook and stir onions in butter until tender. Spoon onion mixture evenly over biscuits. Sprinkle with pepper.

Bake at 375°F for 12 to 15 minutes or until biscuits are golden brown.

Ham and Cheese Crescent Pockets

Yield: 4 servings

- 4 *thin slices cooked ham*
- 4 *thin slices Cheddar cheese*
- 1 *(8-oz.) can Pillsbury Refrigerated Crescent Dinner Rolls*

Heat oven to 375°F. Separate dough into 4 rectangles; firmly press perforations to seal. On unbuttered cookie sheet, press or roll each to form 7x5-inch rectangle. Place one ham slice and one cheese slice on each rectangle. For each rectangle, fold dough in half over filling; press edges firmly to seal.

Bake at 375°F for 10 to 13 minutes or until golden brown.

Cheese Steak Crescent Braid

Yield: 6 servings

- 4 *portions frozen, thinly sliced sandwich steaks, cut crosswise into ½-inch wide strips*
- 2 *tablespoons butter*
- 1 *medium onion, chopped (½ cup)*
- 1 *large green bell pepper, cut into strips (1½ cups)*
- ¼ *teaspoon salt*
- ⅛ *teaspoon pepper*
- 2 *(8-oz.) cans Pillsbury Refrigerated Crescent Dinner Rolls*
- 4 *ounces (1 cup) shredded Mozzarella cheese*
- 1 *egg, beaten, if desired*

Heat oven to 350°F. In large skillet over medium-high heat, stir-fry steaks in butter until no longer pink; remove from skillet. Add onion and green pepper; cook until crisp-tender, about 5 minutes. Return cooked steak to skillet; stir in salt and pepper.

Unroll 1 can dough into 2 long rectangles on ungreased cookie sheet. Overlap long sides to form 13x7-inch rectangle; firmly press perforations and edges to seal. Spoon 1 heaping cup meat mixture in 2-inch wide strip lengthwise down center of rectangle. Sprinkle 1/2 cup of the cheese over meat. Make cuts 1 inch apart on each side of the rectangle just to edge of filling. To give braided appearance, fold strips of dough at an angle halfway across filling, alternating from side to side. Fold ends of braid under to seal. On second ungreased cookie sheet, repeat using remaining can of dough, meat mixture and cheese. Brush braids with beaten egg.

Bake at 350°F for 16 to 22 minutes or until golden brown. Cool slightly; remove from cookie sheet. Cool 5 minutes before serving.

Tuna Pasta Primavera Soup

Yield: 4 (1 cup) servings

- 2 *cups water*
- 1 *(1-lb.) pkg. Green Giant® Pasta Accents® Primavera Frozen Vegetables and Pasta*
- 1 *(5-oz.) can PET® Evaporated Milk*
- 1 *(6½-oz.) can water-packed tuna, drained, flaked*

In medium saucepan, combine water, frozen vegetables and pasta and milk. Bring to a boil. Reduce heat; simmer 10 minutes or until pasta is tender, stirring occasionally. Stir in tuna. Cook 2 to 3 minutes or until thoroughly heated. If desired, sprinkle with salt and pepper.

Chicken and Pasta in Cajun Cream

Szechuan Pork and Pasta Stir-Fry

Yield: 4 (1¾ cup) servings

- 3 *ounces (1½ cups) uncooked bow-tie pasta*
- 1 *tablespoon butter*
- 1 *pound boneless pork, cut into 2x¼x¼-inch strips*
- 1 *(1 lb. 5-oz.) pkg. Green Giant® Create a Meal!® Frozen Szechuan Stir-fry Meal Starter*

Cook pasta to desired doneness as directed on package; drain. Meanwhile, heat butter in large skillet over medium-high heat until hot. Add pork; cook and stir 3 to 5 minutes or until no longer pink. Add frozen vegetables and sauce from packet; set peanuts in packet aside. Cover; cook 6 minutes, stirring every 2 minutes.

Stir in pasta. Cook, uncovered, until mixture comes to a boil and vegetables are crisp-tender. Sprinkle with peanuts from packet.

Vegetable Topped Microwave-Baked Potatoes

Microwave freshly scrubbed potatoes. Top baked potatoes with your favorite cooked Green Giant® frozen vegetables in cheese flavored sauce.

Chicken and Pasta in Cajun Cream

Yield: 3 (1½ cup) servings

- 1 to 2 *tablespoons butter*
- 2 *boneless skinless chicken breast halves, cut into ½-inch pieces*
- 1 *cup red bell pepper strips (2x¼x¼-inch)*
- ½ *cup chopped green onions*
- 1 *(1-lb.) pkg. Green Giant® Pasta Accents® Garlic Seasoning Frozen Vegetables with Pasta*
- ½ *cup whipping cream or half-and-half*
- 1 *teaspoon cumin*
- ¼ to ½ *teaspoon salt*
- ¼ to ½ *teaspoon ground red pepper (cayenne)*

Heat butter in large skillet over medium-high heat until hot. Add chicken; cook and stir 2 to 4 minutes or until no longer pink. Add bell pepper strips, chopped green onions and frozen vegetables with pasta. Cook 4 minutes or until pasta is tender, stirring occasionally. Stir in cream, cumin, salt and ground red pepper. Reduce heat to medium-low; cover and cook 5 minutes or until vegetables are crisp-tender. Spoon mixture onto serving platter; garnish with bell pepper rings and onion fans, if desired.

Fiesta Style Sloppy Joes!

Yield: 5 servings

- 1 *(10.8-oz.) can Pillsbury GRANDS!® Refrigerated Buttermilk Biscuits*
- 1 *pound ground beef*
- 1 *small onion, chopped*
- 1 *(11-oz.) can Green Giant® Mexicorn® Whole Kernel Corn, Red and Green Peppers*
- 1 *(10¾-oz.) can condensed tomato soup*
- ¼ *cup water*
- 1¼ *teaspoon chili powder*
- ⅛ to ¼ *teaspoon hot pepper sauce*

Heat oven to 375°F. Bake biscuits as directed on can. Meanwhile, in large skillet brown beef and onion; drain. Stir in remaining ingredients. Bring to a boil. Reduce heat; cover and simmer 10 minutes or until thoroughly heated. To serve, split warm biscuits; place 2 halves on each plate. Spoon hot beef mixture over biscuit halves.

Sausage and Pasta Skillet

SAUSAGE AND PASTA SKILLET

Yield: 4 (1¼ cup) servings

- 4 *ounces (1¼ cups) uncooked wagon wheel pasta*
- ¾ *pound bulk pork sausage*
- 1 *(10-oz.) pkg. Green Giant® Frozen Broccoli, Cauliflower and Carrots in Cheese Flavored Sauce*

Cook pasta to desired doneness as directed on package. Drain; keep warm. Meanwhile, cook vegetables in sauce as directed on package. Brown sausage in large skillet over medium heat; drain. Add pasta and cooked vegetables to skillet; toss gently.

GREEN BEAN AND TURKEY CASSEROLE

Yield: 4 to 6 servings

- 1½ to 2 *cups leftover cubed cooked turkey or chicken*
- 1 *(10¾ oz.) can cream of mushroom soup*
- 1 *(14.5 oz.) can Green Giant® Cut Green Beans, drained*
- 1 *cup (4 oz.) shredded Cheddar cheese*
- ⅓ *cup milk*
- 6 *servings Hungry Jack® Mashed Potatoes, prepared as directed on package*
- ½ *can french fried onion rings*

In 2 quart casserole, combine turkey, soup, green beans, cheese and milk. Microwave on HIGH for 5 to 6 minutes or until mixture is hot and bubbly, stirring once halfway through cooking.

Top with prepared mashed potatoes; sprinkle with onion rings. Microwave on HIGH for 2 to 3 minutes until mixture is hot and bubbly.

TACO AND BLACK BEAN SKILLET DINNER

Yield: 5 (1½ cup) servings

- 1 *(24-oz.) jar Old El Paso® Thick 'N Chunky Salsa or Picante*
- 1 *(4.6-oz.) pkg. Old El Paso® Taco Shells (12 shells)*
- 4 *ounces (1 cup) shredded Monterey Jack cheese*
- 4 *ounces (1 cup) shredded Cheddar cheese*
- 1 *small onion, chopped (¼ cup)*
- 1 *(11-oz.) can Green Giant® White Corn, drained*
- 1 *(4.5-oz.) can Old El Paso® Chopped Green Chiles*
- 1 *(19-oz.) can Progresso® Black Beans or 15-oz. can Green Giant® or Joan of Arc® Black Beans, drained*
- 2 *teaspoons cumin*
- 1 *tablespoon steak sauce*

Garnish

- ½ to 1 *cup sour cream*
- *Fresh cilantro sprigs*
- *Chopped fresh tomatoes, if desired*
- *Sliced ripe olives, if desired*
- *Chopped jalapeño chiles, if desired*
- *Guacamole, if desired*

Spray deep 10-inch skillet with nonstick cooking spray. Spread 1 cup of the salsa over bottom of sprayed skillet. Break each taco shell into 4 to 6 pieces. Arrange half of the broken shells over salsa. Spread 1 cup of the remaining salsa over shells. Sprinkle with 1/2 cup each of the Monterey Jack cheese and Cheddar cheese. Top with onion, corn and green chilies.

In small bowl, combine beans, cumin and steak sauce; mix well. Spoon evenly over mixture in skillet. Top with remaining broken shells, Monterey Jack cheese and Cheddar cheese and salsa. Cover; cook over medium-low heat for 15 to 20 minutes or until mixture is bubbly and cheese is melted.

To serve, top with 1/2 cup of the sour cream; garnish with cilantro, tomatoes, olives, jalapeño chilies and guacamole. If desired, serve with remaining 1/2 cup sour cream.

I. Appetizers

★

II. Main Courses

★

III. Breakfast Selections
(see also Muffins/Breads/Biscuits)

★

IV. Soups/Stews/Chowders

★

V. Vegetables/Salads/Side Dishes

★

VI. Desserts

★

VII. Muffins/Breads/Biscuits

★

VIII. Flavored Butters

★

★